"Dr. Mike Harris is a thoughtful and dedicated activist whose passion and creativity are clearly woven throughout the pages of this book. This book is an invaluable handbook for those who want to counter the pernicious lies being promoted by anti-Israel activists. It not only debunks their arguments, it also gives you techniques you can use to make your points most effectively. Whether you're fighting against an Israel boycott effort in your community, or an Israel divestment resolution on campus, 'Winning a Debate with an Israel-Hater' can help you tremendously."

--Roz Rothstein, CEO and Co-founder of StandWithUs

WINNING A DEBATE WITH AN ISRAEL-HATER

SECOND EDITION

WINNING A DEBATE WITH AN ISRAEL-HATER:

How to Effectively Challenge Anti-Israel Extremists in Your Neighborhood

Second Edition

Dr. Michael Harris

Published 2018 by Shorehouse Books
Printed in the United States of America

ISBN 0-9994127-9-5
EAN-13 978-0-9994127-9-4

Dedication

**To the memories of my father Hal Harris
and my father-in-law Samson Inwald, who
were both dedicated to the country and
people of Israel.**

Introduction to the Second Edition:

What? We still need to be doing this? Sadly, yes. Somehow, the first edition of <u>Winning a Debate with an Israel Hater</u> failed to neutralize all those who are dedicated to the elimination of the one Jewish state on the globe. So the Elders of the International Zionist Conspiracy demanded an update.

Though really, not much has happened since October 2015, right? Hamas still controls Gaza, and though it hasn't launched another full-scale missile war, it has attempted to invade across the border with armed jihadi fighters masquerading, unconvincingly, as "unarmed peaceful protestors." Mahmoud Abbas is in the 14th year of his 4 year term as President of the Palestinian Authority, and continues to tirelessly negotiate with the UN and the EU (though not with Israel) in support of a two state solution (as long as neither one is a Jewish state). Iran, now enriched with cash from the JCPOA (the nuclear "deal" with the West), still props up the murderous Assad regime in Syria, underwrites Hezbollah's growing missile inventory, and now sends cash to Hamas as well. Iran also continues to develop and test ballistic missiles for the nuclear weapons it claims not to be building. Anti-Israel groups on university campuses continue to put Israel on kangaroo-court trial under the guise of debating BDS (boycott, divestment and sanctions) resolutions; such debates are often followed by anti-Semitic incidents, demonstrating the effects of the demonization of Israel that is an indispensable feature of advocating for BDS. The UN's efforts continue to be UNhelpful, UNproductive, and certainly far from UNbiased.

Oh wait. Something did happen. The small matter of a presidential election in the US that has dramatically affected the conversation about Israel in both positive and negative ways. When <u>Winning a Debate with an Israel Hater</u> was published, the odds that Donald Trump would be elected President in 2016 were sitting at around 5%. Now we have an Administration that supports Israel in unreservedly positive language that up until now has been, so to speak, un-presidented. But—is it really good for the Jewish state? We'll dive into that in Chapter 12.

We've also seen an openly anti-Zionist extremist, Jeremy Corbyn, take control of the Labour Party in the UK. The prevalence of anti-Semitism, including Rothschild conspiracy theories and Holocaust denial, among his supporters demonstrates yet again that anti-Zionism is the more politically correct front for anti-Semitism. And demonstrates yet again that demonizing Jews in Jerusalem and Tel Aviv leads inexorably to demonizing Jews in New York and London.

I'm glad you're joining me on this challenging journey. I'm also delighted to have this edition include cartoons from Zionist Pugs™ (www.zionistpugs.com)! PS: The Pug tells me that special Zionist swag might be appearing soon on that site.

If you enjoy this book, please let the Elders know. Maybe one day they'll actually send me that truckload full of shekels that members of the International Zionist Conspiracy are constantly accused of receiving.....

Acknowledgements

As a new author, I embarked on this effort with no small measure of trepidation. You would not be reading this book without invaluable guidance given to me by Dan Kurtzman, whose books "How to Win a Fight with a Liberal" and "How to Win a Fight with a Conservative" inspired this project. I also benefited from skillful editing by Josh Chetwynd and by Roz Warren.

Philippe Assouline was generous in allowing me to use his "Palestinese Lexicon."

Dusty Katz has contributions all through the text, and has not only my thanks but my deep admiration.

Sharon Cohn provided essential and ongoing encouragement.

My wife Barbara and my children Ben and Molly supplied support, patience and tolerance not only for this project, but for the many hours I spend advocating for Israel. Barbara also compiled the index for the book.

I wish Dan Kliman and Ross Meltzer were here to read this. They both left us far too soon. I hope they would have enjoyed it.

Maya Ilyashov created the cover art that perfectly matches the spirit of the book.

Table of Contents

Preface

It often happens in the middle of an otherwise pleasant day; you're shopping, or walking across a college campus -- and you encounter them. They're holding signs that claim Israel is an "apartheid state" and charge Israel with committing "genocide" against Palestinians. They're calling for boycotts against Israeli products, and divestment from companies that do business with Israel.

You know supporting Israel is the right thing to do. And you're not alone. For decades, polls have shown a large plurality, usually a majority, of Americans back Israel. But here's the problem: you don't know how to respond – or if you even should – to these Israel haters.

This is an all-too-familiar sight, and has become more frequent in the past several decades as Israel-bashing extremists have taken their hostility into the public square. Their words don't represent a simple disagreement with specific actions or policies of the Israeli government. Instead, they're an open call for the elimination of the one country that shares American values in a region full of despots and anti-American fanatics. Simply put, they're not just promoting a Palestinian state; they're demanding that it replace the Jewish one.

Most Americans who want to champion Israel don't know the facts of the situation well enough to counter the lies. They're not equipped with techniques that can unmask the underlying agenda of those who I'll refer to as the People with

Israel Derangement Syndrome (PIDS), a term that has been flying around the internet for at least a decade. These individuals and groups openly, proudly, and viciously attack Israel for its very existence as the nation of the Jewish people. And while these haters are aware that there are comprehensive sources of information available to defeat their agenda, they are banking on those resources being too dry and too daunting for the average, overworked American or busy college student to use effectively.

That's where this book comes in. Imagine some of the key points from Alan Dershowitz's authoritative volume, The Case For Israel-- as it might be delivered by Bill Maher. All the information you need in this street fight of words, but delivered in a light and accessible way, with satirical humor.

This isn't meant to be the definitive guide, but rather a valuable primer. It's the product of years of personal experience dealing with PIDS in and around San Francisco, which is a flashpoint battleground over this issue. Israel's Reut Institute has identified the Bay Area as one of five worldwide "hubs of delegitimization" of Israel. As one of the founders in 2004 of a grassroots group, San Francisco Voice for Israel— which is now the Bay Area chapter of StandWithUs, an international Israel education organization based in Los Angeles-- I have years of experience talking to people about Israel in the San Francisco Bay Area. I've spoken in synagogues, in churches, and out in public on the street, often countering demonstrations by anti-Israel groups. I've seen the half-truths and the lies that the PIDS proffer onto an unsuspecting public, and I've learned how to rebut them. These pages are a distillation of those experiences, in the expectation that you will find them useful yourself.

This book won't explain why Israel should be important to you; if you've picked it up, I assume that it already is. (Either that, or you're just hanging out in the "politics" section of the bookstore to look cool.) If you need an explanation of why the Jewish people want, require and deserve our own country in a portion of our historic homeland, I recommend <u>Why I Am A Zionist</u> by Gil Troy, <u>The Promise of Israel</u> by Daniel Gordis, and <u>Letters to My Palestinian Neighbor</u> by Yossi Klein Halevi. .

This book will teach you how to effectively respond. To those who put on their keffiyeh scarves and call for boycotts against Israel, while they remain strangely silent about Middle Eastern dictatorships that slaughter Arabs—including Palestinians-- by the hundreds or even thousands. To those seeming supporters of women's rights who spout lies about the one country in that region of the world that most supports those rights. And to, in the words of former Israeli Ambassador to the United Nations Ron Prosor, "[t]hose who think that one Jewish state is one too many."

My goal is to empower, enlighten, and, hopefully, entertain. So next time you see a group of PIDS, you'll be armed with the facts – and the techniques to apply them with skill and confidence.

Chapter 1: Winning the Debate

Zionist Pugs

It is impossible to defeat an ignorant man in argument. -- attributed to William McAdoo, industrialist, lawyer and politician

The rhetorical battles waged over Israel are like guerilla warfare. It's often hard to know if you're winning. Not only that, People with Israel Derangement Syndrome (PIDS) are so biased against Israel that earning a "win" in the sense of changing your opponent's mind is almost impossible.

(Wait—don't put this book down and demand your money back—not yet, anyway.)

It's difficult to win a debate:

--with someone who thinks that an ethnically-based state is a problem if it is Jewish... but not if it is Egyptian, Syrian,

Irish, Italian-- or Palestinian. Or with someone who claims that he opposes all ethnically-based nation states, but whose political activism against them starts (and ends) with the Jewish one.

--with someone who thinks that a state for Jews is unacceptable because it is based on religion, but that fifty-seven members of the Organization of Islamic Cooperation, many of which explicitly adopt Sharia law as the basis of their legal system, aren't problematic.

--with someone who believes that the Palestinian issue is the paramount "human rights" issue in a world where a militant Islamic movement publicized its beheadings and crucifixions of "infidels" and sought to wipe out entire indigenous populations, where China brutally oppresses Tibetans, where children in Africa are forced into armed combat, and where women and girls in many countries are subjected to honor killings and female genital mutilation

-- with someone who is relentless in his determination to ignore any facts that don't fit into the worldview of "Israel= racist colonial oppressor; Palestinians= noble indigenous oppressed people."

And when you encounter Israel-haters in any of their various guises—whether it is the aging hippie-needing-a-cause or the young far-out-leftist—and you do try to engage them in conversation, it proves to be as effective as enrolling a cat in obedience school.

So how do you "win?" And why engage in these discussions at all? Because the PIDS are not your target audience!

In society, whether you are interacting with folks face to face or in cyberspace, you will encounter three kinds of people:

1. Those who completely oppose the existence of Israel as the state of the Jewish people

2. A much larger number who actively support Israel

3. And, far bigger than both groups, the majority who don't have strong opinions about this issue and usually aren't paying much attention to it at all, except when it is brought to their attention by a flare-up of violence in the region, an action on the local university campus, or a demonstration in their community.

And this group, not your interlocutor, is the audience that you are trying to reach.

Your audience walks around campus, listens to the radio, reads the letters to the editor sections of newspapers and magazines, and browses all over cyberspace—even the comment sections of online news sites and blogs. On any given day, scan "Google News" for the topic "Israel." Not only will you see actual news reports, but you will also find as top search results Huffington Post/Daily Beast blog posts, and even anti-Israel letters to the editor in local newspapers. (Memo to the allegedly Jewish-controlled media: fix that problem already! What's taking so long?)

Most of this audience does support Israel over the Palestinians when the question is posed as to which side they support more. According to Gallup polls since 2003, this support for Israel runs consistently at 55-70% compared to 15-20% for the Palestinians. But recently, the public has been exposed to a relentless campaign of half-truths and outright lies, far too often reported by media that is either too lazy or too gullible to question the outrageous statements that they publicize.

So how do we define "winning?" You're not going to have people holding up signs to score your debating finesse. (What? Only a 6.5 from the Russian judge??) You're not going to get a medal for your performance from the International Zionist Conspiracy (at least that's what they instructed me to say). And you're not going to get a member of the local branch of Students for Justice in Palestine to step back and say, "Whoa! I never thought of that! You're right," before slinking off in utter mortification. (Actually, if you use the techniques here and this does happen, I'll be happy to take credit. Or cash.)

But even if you can't earn a decisive victory, you don't want to be afraid to engage and challenge anti-Israel activism. Perhaps you'll get the haters to think twice, but even if you don't, you have an opportunity to reach the same audience that they're trying to recruit. And doing so with the facts and satirical weapons offered throughout this book will give you a strong advantage in this clash of ideas.

What you might accomplish is getting a fair-minded person, who is listening to the exchange, to think more about what you have to say. You might get them to realize that the steady drumbeat of misinformation from the other side might not reflect the reality of a complex ethno-religious conflict that is over a century old. You might even get them to engage in conversation with you, to ask you some genuine questions, and to reconsider some of what they have heard. (Note: if there are no fair-minded people in the vicinity, it might be best to back away slowly and pick a different time to practice what you'll learn here!)

Why does this matter? Because the more that Americans think about this conflict, the more they side with Israel. This Gallup poll taken in August 2014, during the middle of Operation Pillar of Defense, shows a striking correlation between learning about the issue and support for Israel:

Views of Israeli and Hamas Actions by Use of Specific Media to Follow News of the Middle East Conflict

	Israeli actions mostly justified	Hamas actions mostly justified
	%	%
National adults	42	14
Read or seen a lot or some news about conflict on television and cable news	55	15
Read or seen a lot or some news about conflict on Internet	53	18
Read or seen a lot or some news about conflict in newspapers	54	14
Read or seen a lot or some news about conflict on Facebook, Twitter, or other social media	49	18

Aug 2-3, 2014

This book won't address a different type of discussion—that which takes place constantly among those who acknowledge the right of the Jewish people to its own nation-state in a portion of its historic homeland. Those conversations relate to criticism or support of specific leaders, policies and actions of the State of Israel. While those discussions are vital, interesting and often extremely vigorous, both within Israel and abroad, they are not the focus of this book. Instead, I will focus on how to respond to the People with Israel Derangement Syndrome, who completely reject Israel's right to exist and campaign for its destruction.

This is not to reduce the entire spectrum of opinion on this volatile issue to a binary choice between "Israel right or wrong" and "Palestine from the river to the sea" (the chant at any demonstration of PIDS, calling for a Palestinian state in the entire area between the Jordan River and the Mediterranean Sea, and a Jewish state, well, nowhere). Nor is it to overlook the enormous amount of nuanced opinion that does-- and should-- exist regarding Israel, and which can be the subject of thoughtful and interesting dialogue between well-meaning people. Rather, it's to help you demonstrate how the PIDS are so extreme that they deserve to be ridiculed and marginalized, because they are not well-meaning, at least with regard to Israel. Their pathological rejection of the Jewish state should be considered part of the great toxic waste dump of other political philosophies based on hatred, a place that can be researched if you wear the appropriate HazMat suit but otherwise is best left alone.

(source: Mohammed Ouda/Wikimedia Commons)

So why then are we deliberately going to wade into it?

• Because while you know that you support Israel and understand the right of the Jewish people to national self-determination, you don't know how to respond to the assertion that millions of Palestinians also have a right to live in the cities and villages which their grandparents or great-grandparents left—for various reasons--in 1948.

• Because you hear statements that Israel is required under international law to give up all of the territory it conquered in 1967, but you don't know how to refute them.

• Because you want to see genuine peace between Israelis and Palestinians, but you don't know how to counter the argument that "one democratic state" between the Jordan River and the Mediterranean Sea is the way to achieve it.

• Because you are offended by Christian church leaders who side with militant Islamists against the one country in the Middle East where the recognized Christian population is not oppressed but, rather, is growing.

• Because you are outraged by supporters of LGBT rights and women's rights who virulently slander the one country in that region of the world that most supports those rights.

Photo courtesy of Miroslav Marinov (Blogwrath.com)

(Imagine a Pride Parade in Gaza!)

• Because when you hear or read lies from those who hate the very existence of a Jewish state, you want to be able to respond effectively and hold them accountable. According to

Manfred Gerstenfeld's book <u>Demonizing Israel and the Jews</u> they have managed to get over 150 million Europeans to believe that Israel is "exterminating" the Palestinians. You don't want to see them successfully selling that malignant myth in your neighborhood.

You don't want to slink away, but you don't know how to start challenging their invective. This book is here to help. I'll give you the information you need to provide some perspective on the picture being painted by the PIDS, which looks like this:

and allow you to reveal the rest of the picture so the view is both visually and morally clearer:

I'll give you a basic primer on the key issues, plus a field-tested technique that will rhetorically pull the rug out from under your opponent. I'll show you how to help your opponent paint himself or herself into that small foul-smelling corner of the political spectrum labeled "extremist."

This is not meant to be anything more than a starting point for your own self-education about Israel. You will want to learn more about all of these issues, because your knowledge will be the best tool to prove how ill-informed--or deliberately wrong-- the PIDS are.

I'm not going to promote the specific policies of whatever democratically elected government is currently in power in Israel. You can disagree with its statements and its actions, while simultaneously supporting the right of the Jewish state to elect its own leadership and determine its own future. While many people were opposed to policies of Barack Obama on the one hand or Donald Trump on the other, almost none of them were suggesting that the very existence of the United States is illegitimate because of the choices either one of them made, or the choices that millions of Americans made in voting for them. And, quite honestly, the PIDS don't care whether Israel has a right-leaning Likud government or a left-leaning Labor government. They don't accept that there should be such an entity as "the government of Israel" at all. They'll try to claim that they're just "opposed to Israeli government policy", but in fact there isn't any policy that Israel can adopt, short of national suicide, that they will accept. (And possibly not even that one...)

You'll notice the use of humor in this book. It could be the reason you're reading it—if you want a serious tome by a respected author, there are comprehensive books like The Case for Israel by Alan Dershowitz and Myths and Facts by Dr. Mitchell Bard.

Of course, the Israeli-Arab conflict is not a laughing matter at all—the various wars have produced thousands of deaths, over a million refugees, and the rise of modern stateless terrorist organizations, both secular and Islamist, whose openly stated goal is to continue the conflict against Israel forever. And I'm not making light of what is, literally, a deadly serious issue.

But if humor will get you to turn the pages, then I invite you to join me on our journey through this conflict. Fasten your seat belt, and keep your wits about you at all times.

Key Points:

Your audience is not the PIDS, who can't be convinced by facts, but rather those who are watching the debate.

Knowledge is power—the more people know, the more they support Israel

Chapter 2: A Dash Through History

You may ask yourself, well, how did I get here? --Talking Heads, Once in a Lifetime

Any discussion of Israel requires understanding the story of the modern state—the rise of Zionism, the founding of the state, and its brief but incredibly eventful history. Your knowledge of the key events that led to the rebirth of the Jewish state in the Jewish homeland will enable you to refute the lies that the PIDS will present about them. And as you will see, all the activism of the PIDS is aimed at delegitimizing the very existence of the Jewish state. Put briefly, it's not about 1967, when Israel took control of the eastern part of Jerusalem as well as Judea and Samaria (known after 1948 as the "West Bank") which had been previously occupied by Jordan; the Gaza Strip, which had been occupied by Egypt, and the Golan Heights, which had been part of Syria; it's about 1947, when the United Nations endorsed the partition of the British Mandate of Palestine into Jewish and Arab states. It's not only about Israelis in Judea and Samaria; it's just as much about Israelis in Tel Aviv.

(Note that the use of the term "West Bank" legitimizes Jordan's 19 year occupation, while erasing 30 centuries of Jewish history in that same area. This was, historically, the heart of the indigenous Jewish homeland; the name "Jew" refers to the people of Judea. In this edition, I will use the more legitimate historical name except when referring solely to the Arab population of this area.)

What follows is a brief chronology of events that you need to be familiar with. Keep in mind that the history of the Jews in the Land of Israel starts long before this. As the historian Barbara Tuchman wrote, Israel is "the only nation that is governing itself in the same territory, under the same name, and with the same religion and same language as it did three thousand years ago."[1]

Our history began 3000 years ago, and was already 1000 years old when the Romans destroyed the Second Temple in 70 AD. It is literally carved into the land, having been unearthed by archaeologists who have revealed evidence of the Jewish kingdoms going back to First Temple times, 2600 years ago, which means that the history of modern Israel is really the story of the return of the Jewish people to their homeland. Any discussion of Israel must be framed this way—that the Jews, the

---

[1] Tuchman, Barbara W. Practicing History: Selected Essays. Random House, 2014

oldest remaining indigenous inhabitants of the land of Israel, were returning to their ancestral territory, and that this return had been taking place for hundreds of years before the rise of modern Zionism. This was a unique situation in recorded history: a people who had been exiled from the land in which their history began, and faced with discrimination and genocide in almost all other lands, was finally returning to the home for which, and towards which, they had prayed for centuries.

The PIDS will often describe Israel as a "settler-colonial" state, as if the Jews leaving Europe were coming to a land foreign to their history. But the Land of Israel is the place where the Jewish people developed a nation, a religion and a unique language. The Arabs, on the other hand, forged their national identity, religion and language in the Arabian Peninsula. They then exported these across the Middle East by conquest, 1500 years after the establishment of the Jewish kingdoms. The Arabic language and the religion of Islam are no more indigenous to the Levant (or North Africa) than the Spanish language and Roman Catholicism are to Latin America; both are the result of a colonial-imperial enterprise that imposed them on the native populations. Put briefly (and in rhyme!): Jews are from Judea, Arabs are from Arabia.

1880s-1890s: First Aliyah (a Hebrew term which means "going up," used to describe Jews moving back to the Land of Israel). Russian Jews, fleeing pogroms and persecution, establish new communities in the land of Israel, then ruled by the Ottoman Empire as part of the vilayet (province) of Beirut. There is no such entity as "Palestine" at this time; the name, applied by the Romans after they suppressed the revolt led by Bar Kochba in the year 135, only comes back into general use in the 20th century. Land for these immigrants is purchased, often from absentee landlords, under the laws of the Ottoman Empire.

These Russian Jews join a Jewish population that has been continuously living in the region for 3000 years, descendants of the Jewish nation-- the only self-governing nation ever to arise in that region of the Middle East. PIDS will often claim that the Jews co-existed in peace with the Muslim population at the time. That is true only if you consider living as a second class citizen (a dhimmi) under Muslim law, subjected to discriminatory taxes and frequent murderous pogroms, to be "peaceful co-existence."

1896: Herzl. Theodor Herzl, an Austrian Jewish journalist who was galvanized by the Dreyfus affair in France, publishes "Der Judenstaat" ("The Jewish State") which calls for the establishment of a state of, and for, the Jewish people. Herzl recognizes that assimilation of secular Jews in Europe did not solve the problem of anti-Semitism, and believes that the only way to successfully respond is to have the Jewish people exercise their own rights as a nation in their own homeland. This is the essence of Zionism. (The PIDS have made Zionism an epithet, and try to identify it in the public mind with the most extreme elements of Israeli society. We need to reclaim the word as a right, one that we assert with just as much legitimacy as any other indigenous people can.)

1897: The First Zionist Congress meets in Basel, Switzerland and adopts a program calling for the establishment of a home for the Jewish people in the land of Israel.

1904-1914: The Second Aliyah, mostly Russian Jews, sees tens of thousands of Jews immigrate into the area, including many socialists who founded the first kibbutzim (collective farms).

1914: The Ottoman Empire joins the Central Powers against the Allies in World War I.

1917: As the British Army under General Allenby closes in on Jerusalem, British Foreign Secretary Arthur Balfour issues a letter to Lord Rothschild, head of the Jewish community in Britain, committing British support for "the establishment in Palestine of a national home for the Jewish people." This letter becomes known as the Balfour Declaration.

1920: Treaty of Sevres. The Allies and the Ottoman Empire sign a treaty which includes provisions for the dismemberment of the Ottomans' former holdings in the Middle East, resurrecting Roman-area appellations that had not been used for centuries such as "Libya," "Syria" and "Palestine." It calls for a British Mandate in Palestine to develop a national home for the Jewish people, as well as a British Mandate in Iraq (an entirely new concoction that was cobbled together out of Sunni, Shiite and Kurdish areas) and French Mandates in Syria (another newly synthesized nation) and Lebanon (designed as an enclave for Maronite Christians) to lead those areas to independence.

(Yet the right of Iraq and Syria to exist as independent states, even when ruled by brutal tyrants that slaughter both citizens and foreigners by the thousands, remains unquestioned today. The Jewish state? That's a different story, which is why you picked up this book, isn't it?)

1922: The British unilaterally separate the area known as Trans-Jordan (now the country of Jordan) from the Palestine Mandate, which is then formally approved by the League of Nations.

1929: Arab Terrorism. Massacres against Jewish civilians are committed in Hebron and elsewhere in Palestine, instigated by Haj Amin al-Husseini, the British-appointed Grand Mufti of Jerusalem. The rioters in Hebron chant "itbach el-Yahud" (Arabic for "kill the Jew") and kill dozens of members of that Jewish community—the oldest Jewish community in the world, dating back to Biblical times. The rest flee to other Jewish communities in Palestine. This was the first example in 20th century Palestine of ethnic cleansing of Jews by Arabs. It would not be the last.

1936-1939: The Great Arab Revolt. Arabs launch widespread attacks on both the British Mandatory government and Jewish civilians. The Grand Mufti consolidates his own political power by murdering members of rival families who are more accepting of coexistence with the Jews. During the Revolt, the British send a commission led by Lord Peel to recommend steps to end the violence. The commission recommends partition of Palestine into a small Jewish state and a much larger Arab state, with Jerusalem remaining under British control (see map below). The Arabs reject this plan, marking their first refusal to accept the creation of the first-ever Palestinian state. Jewish opinion is divided. Ultimately, the British abandon the plan.

The Peel Plan, 1937.
Map courtesy of The-Jewish-Story.org

During the Revolt, the Mufti subsequently flees Palestine and helps incite the 1941 Farhud pogrom in Baghdad against that city's large Jewish community. He ends up in Berlin where he meets with Hitler, makes radio broadcasts to incite Arabs to join the Nazi cause, and works with Himmler to help plan the extermination of the Jewish community of Palestine. Only the British defeat of Rommel at El Alamein in 1942 prevented him from carrying out this plan.

1939: The White Paper. To appease the Arabs, the British issue the White Paper, which limits Jewish immigration into Palestine to 15,000 per year. By closing off the last recourse for the Jews of Europe, this act seals the fate of millions of Jews who would soon fall under the shadow of Nazi genocide.

By contrast, throughout the Mandatory period (1922-1948), Arab immigration is effectively unrestricted. In 1930, the Hope-Simpson Commission, sent from London to investigate the 1929 Arab riots, concludes that the British practice of ignoring the uncontrolled illegal Arab immigration from Egypt, Transjordan and Syria has the effect of displacing prospective Jewish immigrants.

1945-7: With the defeat of Nazi Germany, the extent of the Holocaust is revealed to the world. Many survivors of genocide, housed in displaced persons camps and with their previous communities eradicated, want to go to Palestine but the British refuse to allow them. Boats such as the "Exodus 1947" attempt to bring the refugees to Palestine; if caught, passengers are imprisoned in Cyprus. Agitation for statehood increases in the Jewish community of Palestine. Some Jews resort to acts of terrorism, most notably the bombing of British headquarters in the King David Hotel in Jerusalem in 1946 by Menachem Begin's Irgun, an underground guerilla force seeking to drive the British out of Palestine. Such attacks are consistently condemned by the leadership of the Yishuv (the Jewish community in Palestine).

1947-8: UN Partition Plan. Increasing violence in Palestine between Jews and Arabs (and between both groups and the British) leads the British to announce that they will return responsibility for the Mandate to the new United Nations, the legal successor to the League of Nations. On November 29, 1947, the General Assembly recommends a plan of partition into "independent Arab and Jewish states" with Jerusalem to remain under international control (see map below). The area assigned to the Jewish state had a Jewish majority. While it included 55% of the land area, most of it was the Negev desert, considered unsuitable for supporting a significant population.

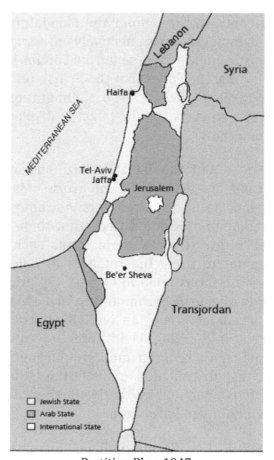

Partition Plan, 1947.
Courtesy of the Israeli Ministry of Foreign Affairs

The Jews of Palestine, through the Jewish Agency led by David Ben-Gurion, immediately accept the plan. The Arabs, through the Arab Higher Committee-- led by the Mufti who had returned to Palestine after the war-- reject peace and a Palestinian state for the second time. The day after the vote, Arab villagers launch attacks on Jewish villages, farms and convoys. Acts of violence by both sides against civilians become infamous. On the Jewish side, the Irgun militia attacks the Arab village of Deir Yassin near Jerusalem on April 9, 1948, resulting in the deaths of more than a hundred Arabs. Four days later, in retaliation, Arab gunmen attack a convoy of doctors and nurses heading towards Hadassah Hospital at Mount Scopus, killing nearly 80. Arabs also lay siege to Jerusalem in an attempt to starve out the city's 100,000 Jews, attacking convoys bringing food and water to the civilian population trapped there. During this time, Arab civilians begin to flee to neighboring areas to avoid the developing war.

May 14, 1948: The British Mandate ends, and in accordance with the UN plan, the Jewish leadership declares the State of Israel, restoring sovereignty over the Jewish homeland to the Jewish people for the first time in 1900 years. The following day, Arab armies from Jordan, Iraq, Lebanon, Egypt and Syria invade. Azzam Pasha, Secretary General of the Arab League, states: "This will be a war of extermination and momentous massacre which will be spoken of like the Tartar massacre or the Crusader wars."

1949: Having successfully fought off the Arabs at a cost of the lives of one out of every 100 Israelis, Israel signs armistice agreements with the neighboring Arab nations. The Arab states, however, refuse to declare peace and recognize Israel, and demanded that the agreements include a clause that they were not recognizing the armistice lines as borders. About 710,000 Arabs have been displaced from the area that becomes the state of Israel; about 150,000 remain and become citizens of Israel. In contrast, no Jews remain alive in the areas that fall under Arab control, except a small number of prisoners of war.

In violation of the UN partition resolution which had called for establishment of an independent Arab state in part of the former Mandate, Egypt continues to occupy the area which becomes known as the Gaza Strip, and Jordan occupies the eastern part of Jerusalem which includes the Old City, as well as Judea and Samaria, the areas that become known as the "West Bank." The armistice line between Israel and Jordan becomes known as the Green Line, for the color of the marker used on what became the official armistice map (see map below).

(Prior to this, neither of these had ever been discrete political or demographic entities. Neither Egypt nor Jordan proposed creating a Palestinian state in those areas. This occupation results in absolutely no international outcry on behalf of the Palestinians.)

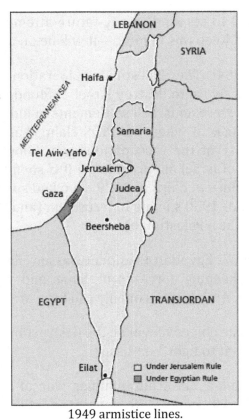

1949 armistice lines.
Courtesy of the Israeli Ministry of Foreign Affairs

1956-57: The Suez Crisis. In a joint operation coordinated with France and Britain, Israel attacks Egypt and conquers the Sinai Peninsula. Egypt's nationalization of the Suez Canal in July of that year led to the French and British involvement. Israel is responding to terror attacks from Egyptian-controlled Gaza as well as the illegal Egyptian blockade of the Straits of Tiran, an international waterway that is the only outlet for Israel's southern port of Eilat. Israel withdraws in March 1957 after the United Nations agrees to install a peacekeeping force in Sinai. The United States also promises Israel to respond to any future attempt to close the Straits of Tiran. Keep this in mind—it will be on the test later.

May 1964: The Palestinian Liberation Organization (PLO), which is sworn to destroy Israel, is founded by the Arab League. (There were no Israeli settlements in Judea, Samaria or Gaza at that time, so when the PIDS claim that the PLO was founded because of the "occupation," you know that they're referring to all of Israel as "occupied.") It is soon taken over by Yasser Arafat, born in Cairo in 1929, who had spent a total of 4 years in the mid- 1930's living in Jerusalem (and the rest of his life claiming to be a Palestinian).

May 1967: Egyptian President Nasser ejects the United Nations peacekeeping force from Sinai and mobilizes the Egyptian Army. Arab leaders openly call for war:

"Our basic objective will be the destruction of Israel. The Arab people want to fight." -- Nasser

"We want a full scale, popular war of liberation... to destroy the Zionist enemy" -- Syrian president Dr. Nureddin al-Attasi

"Our goal is clear - to wipe Israel off the map." -- President Aref of Iraq

Jordan and Syria mobilize their armies on Israel's borders and Jordan places its armed forces under Egyptian command.

Egypt closes the Straits of Tiran again.

The United Nations remains silent. The United States, bogged down in Vietnam, disregards its previous pledge to Israel to defend its freedom of navigation and urges Israel to be patient. (This is where the US, and the rest of the international community, fail that test from 1956.) Israel mobilizes its entire citizen army reserves and thus its economy grinds to a halt.

June 1967: Israel attacks the air forces of Egypt and Syria. Despite assurances from Israel, delivered by United Nations intermediaries, that Israel would not attack Jordan if it stayed out of the conflict, the Jordanians shell Jerusalem. In response, Israeli forces counterattack, capturing Judea and Samaria from Jordan. Israel also goes on to take the Golan Heights from Syria, and Gaza and the Sinai from Egypt (see map below).

Israel and territories conquered in 1967.
Courtesy of the Israeli Ministry of Foreign Affairs

September 1967: the Arab League, meeting in Khartoum, Sudan issues a statement calling for "no peace, no recognition and no negotiation with Israel."

November 1967: the United Nations Security Council adopts Resolution 242, calling for Israel to return territory in exchange for peace. (They obviously didn't get the memo from Khartoum.)

September 1970: Arafat and the PLO instigate a civil war in Jordan and attempt to overthrow Jordan's King Hussein. They also stage international airline hijackings to draw attention to their cause. Hussein defeats the PLO, which then flees to Lebanon.

October 1973: Egyptian and Syrian armies attack Israel on Yom Kippur, the holiest day of the Jewish calendar, triggering a three week war, which ends up as a virtual draw in terms of territory.

November 1977: In a historic and courageous move, Egyptian President Anwar Sadat visits Jerusalem and offers peace between the two countries.

March 1979: Egypt and Israel sign a peace treaty brokered by President Jimmy Carter (who spends the rest of his life betraying that achievement). The agreement includes a framework for Palestinian autonomy. Israel subsequently returns the entire Sinai Peninsula to Egypt.

October 1981: Egyptian President Sadat is assassinated by Islamist soldiers at a military parade in Egypt.

June 1982: After a series of terror attacks by the PLO, Israel invades Lebanon and expels Arafat and PLO troops. (Israel remains in southern Lebanon until it withdraws in 2000.)

1987: Palestinians in the West Bank begin a wave of riots known as the "intifada" (Arabic for "uprising"). It lasts until 1991. Over 1000 Palestinians die as a result of Israeli army responses. A similar number die as a result of intra-Palestinian violence.

September 1993: Israel and the PLO sign the Oslo Agreement, which leads to the establishment of the Palestinian Authority in the West Bank and Gaza. (Photos of the handshake on the White House lawn between Yasser Arafat and Israeli Prime Minister Yitzhak Rabin fail to include the "fingers crossed behind my back" gesture by Arafat.)

November 1995: Prime Minister Rabin is assassinated at a peace rally in Tel Aviv by a right-wing extremist Israeli.

July 2000: At the Camp David Conference between President Bill Clinton, Israeli Prime Minister Ehud Barak and Palestinian leader Yasser Arafat, Barak offers a plan for final peace and the establishment of a Palestinian state. Arafat rejects it. (If you're keeping score, that's three times.)

September 2000: Palestinians begin a wave of terror attacks. Rather than a spontaneous uprising like the first intifada, this was planned by Arafat and other Palestinian Authority leaders immediately after the failure of the Camp David summit. It becomes known as the Second Intifada and lasts until 2005, taking the lives of over 1000 Israelis (over 75% of whom are civilians killed in suicide bombings). Over 4000

Palestinians (two thirds of whom were men of fighting age) die as a result of Israeli military actions during this time.

Photo: Flash 90
Jerusalem bus blown up by suicide bomber, 2002.

March 2002: The Arab League adopts a peace initiative promising to normalize relations with Israel if it completely withdraws from all territories it took over in 1967 and accepts the "right of return" for millions of descendants of Arabs who had become refugees in 1948. The League does not offer to open negotiations, insisting that Israel has to accept the entire proposal as one agreement. (I will return to discussion of this fictional "right of return" in Chapter Six.)

November 2004: Arafat dies in Paris, leaving behind a personal fortune estimated at nearly $1 billion. (International agencies that have delivered billions of dollars in aid to the Palestinians belatedly realize that handing this money directly to Arafat in small unmarked bills might not have been the smartest idea.)

September 2005: Despite strong domestic opposition, Israel withdraws completely from Gaza. Gazans celebrate by immediately destroying agricultural greenhouses left intact by the departing Israelis as a goodwill gesture.

July 2006: The Lebanese terrorist group Hezbollah attacks Israel across the Lebanese border, leading to 34 days of fighting and worldwide protests against "Israeli aggression."

June 2007: Hamas, sworn to destroy Israel as a religious imperative, takes over Gaza from Fatah in a violent coup, removing many Fatah activists from their jobs by throwing them off of tall buildings. Protests against this cold-blooded murder of dozens of Palestinians erupt.... nowhere.

September 2008: Israeli Prime Minister Ehud Olmert makes a peace offer to Palestinian Authority President Mahmoud Abbas offering more concessions than Barak offered to Arafat, and agreeing to divide Jerusalem. Abbas does not accept it. (That's four.)

December 2008: Israel launches Operation Cast Lead in response to Hamas firing thousands of rockets at Israeli towns. In a new technological advance, Hamas now uses rockets that are apparently invisible to Western newspaper headline writers and to self-styled "peace groups."

January 2009: Mahmoud Abbas' four-year term as President of the Palestinian Authority expires. Nobody outside of the pro-Israel community seems to notice.

November 2012: After thousands more of these invisible-to-media-and-leftists rockets are fired from Gaza at

Israeli towns and cities, Israel "breaks the truce with Hamas" and launches Operation Pillar of Defense.

2013-2014: Peace negotiations are held under the auspices of United States Secretary of State John Kerry. Abbas wants to build up Israelis' confidence in his intentions during this process, so he publicly honors dozens of Palestinian murderers who have been released from Israeli prisons. He also insists that he will never recognize Israel as the state of the Jewish people or compromise on the "right of return" for descendants of refugees. Widespread astonishment erupts when these negotiations fail to achieve an agreement.

July-August 2014: following the kidnapping and murder of three Israeli teenagers by Hamas operatives, Hamas increases rocket fire against Israel. Israel responds with Operation Protective Edge, in which an invasion of Gaza leads to the discovery of over twenty tunnels extending under the border with Israel, equipped for terror attacks and kidnappings. Following seven weeks of fighting, which includes several thousand Hamas rocket attacks against Israeli cities, a cease-fire is brokered by Egypt on the same terms that Hamas had rejected on the third day of fighting. Operation Protective Edge also utilizes Israel's Iron Dome missile defense system, which prevents mass civilian casualties on the Israeli side, much to the fury of Hamas supporters.

July 2015: An agreement on Iran's nuclear program was reached with the United States, France, Great Britain, Russia, China and Iran. In exchange for Iran promising not to get caught developing nuclear weapons for 15 years, the other parties agreed to loosen sanctions and allow Iran to repatriate over $100 billion in assets that had been frozen for decades. The Obama Administration assured everyone that Iran would use this money for infrastructure, not to expand its support of terrorism across the region. (Narrator's voice: "They spent the money on terrorism.")

November 8, 2016: Just an ordinary Tuesday, nothing of interest to the US or Israel took place.

April-July 2018: Hamas organizes riots along the 1949 armistice line between Israel and Gaza, using women and children as human shields for attempts to pull down the border fence and invade Israel. Though the overwhelming majority of those killed were Hamas terrorists, Israel is widely condemned for its use of force by the international community, demonstrating once again that they will always uphold Israel's inviolate right to defend its borders (only as long as no Palestinians are harmed in the process).

Key points:

Jews began to return to the land long before the Holocaust.

Arab violence against Jews began before the State of Israel was created.

The conflict began long before the Six Day War in 1967, and the key issue remains the right of Israel to exist as the state of the Jewish people.

Chapter 3: Making Your Points (including the most important statement you can make to neutralize the PIDS)

Zionist Pugs

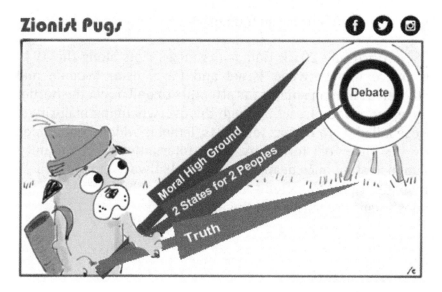

Get up, stand up; stand up for your rights! -- Bob Marley

Before we address how to counter the arguments proffered by the PIDS, we need to address the framework within which you will use them. The most important first step is to define what you stand for and what the other side stands for.

This isn't as obvious as it would seem. The broad (60-70%) range of American support for Israel runs the gamut literally from A to Z: from Americans for Peace Now, which supports a complete Israeli withdrawal from all lands taken over in 1967, to the Zionist Organization of America, which supports ongoing Israeli control of those areas. All of these groups agree that Israel has the right to exist as the state of the Jewish people within secure and defensible borders, but their often vociferous disagreements about everything else dominate not only the Israeli media but also American media, both Jewish and secular, including both old-style newspapers and social media.

Don't let these disagreements obscure the key point:

The Jewish people have just as much right to national self-determination in a portion of our historic homeland as any other people—the Japanese, the Russians, the French, the Turks or the Egyptians—have in theirs.

The PIDS, a small minority of the American public, run the gamut from extremist to wingnut. Some would tolerate the existence of a Jewish minority population in the region and some would not. Some accept and endorse violence against Jews and some do not. Some want to establish a Palestinian state based on Sharia law and others prefer a less medieval form of government. But what they all agree on is that Israel, as the state of the Jewish people, is illegitimate and should be eradicated. Their public discourse doesn't reflect the broad range of opinion that must certainly exist within their movement about "what comes after," because they have put those differences aside for now.

Keep in mind that the PIDS are playing offense (and usually being quite offensive in the process). They are focused on their immediate goal, which is changing the status quo—the existence of Israel, and American support for it. They have the incentive to keep attacking Israel on as many fronts as possible, and they tirelessly throw out a steady stream of half-truths and outright lies, hoping that the constant drumbeat of anti-Israel propaganda will create a tipping point in public opinion.

The other side's shaky relationship with the truth can create problems for us. Just as Hamas or its fellow jihadis can launch 10,000 missiles at Israel hoping that one will get through Israel's Iron Dome defense system and kill dozens of children, the PIDS can launch 10,000 lies at the public, hoping that some will make an impression. They're playing the long game, working to slowly undermine support for Israel, with a goal that eventually—in the next year, next decade or next century—the Jewish state will no longer exist. They're also free to spin any fact (or fiction) to demonize the Jewish state, because in their future scenario, there's no need for Jews and Arabs to live peacefully together—if the Jews don't wish to cooperate with their future Arab overlords, they'll be free to leave (or die trying).

We who support Israel are playing defense—we want Israel to continue to be successful, economically, diplomatically and when necessary, militarily. But we all have different ideas about what Israel should do to bring this about. As Golda Meir once joked, "Israel is a country with three million prime ministers." On a more serious note, historians have noted that bitter internecine conflicts within the Jewish community contributed to the loss of Jerusalem and the destruction of the Temple two thousand years ago.

As Jon Haber points out in his phenomenal "Divest This!" blog (www.divestthis.com), the battle for public opinion on Israel is most akin to siege warfare, and our strategy and tactics need to reflect an understanding of how to successfully weather the siege and ensuring that our opponents' attacks don't cause damage.[2] He points out that while the strategy of the other side involves incessant attacks both on Israel and its supporters, we don't need to engage in that level of destructive hostility on our side. Israel's supporters want to see a Jewish state where Jews and Arabs do live peacefully side by side, and a Middle East where the Jewish state coexists with its Arab neighbors. So it's in Israel's interest, and ours, not to "soil the nest" by portraying all Arabs-- or all Muslims-- as irrevocably evil.

The practical implication is that we must frame the debate in a way that will appeal to the widest range of opinion, take the position that lets us speak from the moral high ground, and make the PIDS declare their extremism openly without letting them hide behind inexact language. This means that we must recognize and support the position of the government of the United States, *and of the government of Israel (as articulated by Prime Minister Netanyahu in 2009)*, which is the "two states for two peoples" formula. This formula provides that the ultimate long-term settlement of the conflict will eventually consist of the withdrawal of Israel from some of Judea and Samaria and the creation in that land of an independent state of Palestine. Now there are many supporters of Israel who disagree with this. However, not only do the majority of Americans support this position, but so do the majority of Israeli Jews across the political spectrum.[3] It also attracts more support

---

[2] http://divestthis.com/2016/06/siege-warfare.html

[3] http://www.jpost.com/DiplomacyAndPolitics/Article.aspx?id=251311, December 2011 poll

among Israeli Jews and Palestinian Arabs than any other option.[4]

Now before my friends on the right side of the political aisle start running for the exits, let me make this clear: I have no expectation that any such agreement will be reached soon. Nor should you. There are profoundly difficult obstacles to be overcome on both sides, the first and foremost being the mulishly obstinate refusal on the part of the Palestinian leadership—since long before 1948, and reiterated during the most recent negotiations— to accept a Jewish state of Israel within any borders at all. Palestinian Authority President Mahmoud Abbas has consistently stood by this rejectionism, even claiming in January 2018 that "Israel is a colonial project that has nothing to do with Jews."[5] Nevertheless, this is the solution toward which we will be heading, however slowly and fitfully, if-- and only if-- the Palestinian leadership ever decides that having a Palestinian state is more important than working for the elimination of Israel. And if the two parties agree on a different arrangement, it certainly won't be one in which the Jewish people, having fought to regain and defend their national sovereignty in their indigenous homeland, decide to renounce it and turn their fate over to others.

When confronted with support for peace between two states for two peoples, the PIDS must stand in opposition. They can't even bring themselves to lie and claim that they would

---

[4] http://www.pcpsr.org/en/node/717

[5] https://www.jta.org/2018/01/15/news-opinion/israel-middle-east/abbas-denies-jewish-connection-to-israel-in-speech-to-palestinian-leadership

support it, because that would require accepting Israel's existence as the state of the Jewish people. Just like the Palestinian leadership over the decades, they are very clear about their intention. Their entire raison d'être is not advocating *for* a Palestinian state, but rather *against* the Jewish one. Students for Justice in Palestine at the University of California at Davis openly admitted this agenda in July 2018: "it is an ideological fantasy to really believe that progress is possible so long as the state of Israel exists."[6]

This means that when we stand up and support peace between two nations, the PIDS are forced into saying "no," thereby supporting ongoing war. Think about the meaning of the "no justice, no peace" mantra that these groups often chant. Some of them openly support terrorism and rocket attacks on Israel, others support "nonviolent" economic and political warfare —but for all of them, the ultimate goal is not to create a Palestinian state to live in peace and mutual recognition alongside Israel, but rather to have a Palestinian state take the place of Israel. And it is vital that we get them to acknowledge this radical position, because it will turn away the majority of Americans who do understand and support the legitimacy of Israel as the state of the Jewish people. Framing the debate as peace versus jihad, while also recognizing the national aspirations of both the Palestinians and the Jews, puts it in terms that the American public understands and agrees with.

---

[6] https://theaggie.org/2018/07/06/students-for-justice-in-palestine-kill-and-expect-love/

This provides you with the single most important point you can make:

"I support a real peace between a Jewish state of Israel and an Arab state of Palestine. What about you?"

The PIDS can only answer "no" (or respond with weasel words such as "we support equal rights for everyone," but always refusing to accept the legitimacy of a Jewish state). And as soon as anyone else hears this, they understand the agenda of the PIDS. If the audience is anywhere near the mainstream of the American political spectrum, they are now on your side.

Here's how straightforward this can be: our local Israel advocacy group was standing with pro-Israel signs and with Israeli flags across the street from an anti-Israel group called Bay Area Women in Black. My sign said "Israel wants peace." A man came over and said (calmly, not threateningly) "I think you have a lot of nerve holding that sign." When I engaged him in conversation, it soon became apparent that while he had strong opinions about some of Israel's actions, he also accepted the Jewish people's right to their own nation. We had a very substantive discussion during which I was able to point out that the people standing across from us did not support Israel's right to exist at all, as well as pointing out some salient facts about Hamas and its goals. He admitted that he hadn't thought about that aspect of the situation, and we shook hands amicably as he left. I don't think he was going to join us in singing "Hatikvah" (Israel's national anthem) anytime soon, but we came to important points of agreement on the core issue. We both agreed that Israel had the right to exist as the state of the Jewish people, and in that regard he was really with us and not with the PIDS across the street. This is the kind of conversation you can have when you stand for peace and the other side stands against it.

Now that you have a position, you need a few methods to communicate your argument effectively. There's a time-tested technique you can use to get your point across—it is called "ARM" (Answer-Reframe-Message). You may have also heard it referred to as "ABC" (Answer-Bridge-Close). Watch any TV news show with spokespeople from two sides of an issue and you will see this in action.

Here's a perfect example. Neil Lazarus, an Israeli political commentator who offers in-depth online public speaking and advocacy training programs at AwesomeSeminars.com, was being interviewed by Britain's Sky TV during Operation Cast Lead (Israel's 2008 action in Gaza). A Palestinian spokesperson claimed that the root of the problem was Israel's occupation. Neil's response was a terrific instance of ARM in action:

Let's get away from the rhetoric of this conflict and look at the facts on the ground. Hamas has taken control of the Gaza Strip. Israel ended the occupation of Gaza, destroyed the settlements and homes of over 9000 Jews, sent our army in and removed those Jews and handed it over to the Palestinians to say 'take control'. Hamas took over and has been sending over 6000 missiles to Israel.

I would ask your viewers one question: if over 6000 missiles were landing in London, Manchester, Leeds; if suicide bombers were sent to Brent Cross or the shopping centers in Manchester, Leeds, Wales, elsewhere, wouldn't the [British] government be doing the same thing?

And your speaker in the studio knows, because he's a Christian, that the Christians in Gaza have also been victims of Hamas. Let's stop this rhetoric and understand that today the problem is a radical organization called Hamas which is a threat to you and me as moderates on the ground. [7]

Neil ARMed the question. He ANSWERED that Israel had ended the occupation of Gaza. He REFRAMED the issue as Hamas' actions. He then delivered his MESSAGE-- that Israel has the right to respond to missiles and that Hamas is the real threat to peace.

In addition to ARM, another method that will help you make your point is the use of anecdotes. US Presidents routinely feature anecdotes in their speeches. In 2012, President Obama's State of the Union address included this one:

Jackie Bray is a single mom from North Carolina who was laid off from her job as a mechanic. Then Siemens opened a gas turbine factory in Charlotte and formed a partnership with Central Piedmont Community College. The company helped the college design courses in laser and robotics training. It paid Jackie's tuition, then hired her to help operate their plant.

I want every American looking for work to have the same opportunity as Jackie did. Join me in a national commitment to train 2 million Americans with skills that will lead directly to a job.

Why do anecdotes work? Because they make an abstract situation real, and allow people to identify with the subject. An

---

[7] http://www.youtube.com/watch?v=PRVVA0tdljc

anecdote speaks to people's emotional responses rather than their intellectual ones—and you can guess which is more effective in motivating public opinion. The PIDS will often reel off names of Palestinians, especially women and children, who were allegedly killed as a result of Israel's actions. Why? Because it is a rhetorical device that works.

We should use this tactic effectively ourselves. As *DivestThis* noted in discussing Israel's incredible humanitarian response to the earthquake in Haiti,

Which of these two statements will stick with you longer?

* Within days of a devastating earthquake striking Haiti, Israel had flown 220 doctors and set up a state-of-the-art mobile field hospital, providing rescue and health services to thousands of people

OR

* Six year old Jessica Hartelin had good reason to believe her life was over after days buried under rubble caused by Haiti's recent earthquake. But she didn't count on courageous local residents pulling her to safety, or on the skill and dedication of Israeli doctors who had set up the only mobile field hospital in the country in order to give local Haitians like Jessica the chance at life.

In the first sentence, Israel helps thousands while in the second it helps only one, and yet the personalization of the story gives the second statement far more rhetorical power (reinforced, not diminished, by the fact that credit for her rescue is given to both Israel and Jessica's Haitian neighbors).[8]

This is such an effective tactic that the PIDS sometimes take it one step further and make up stories, as in the case of the hoax in 2000 regarding the alleged death of a 12-year-old boy, Mohamed al-Durah, by IDF gunfire. The phenomenon of using deliberately mislabeled or edited footage of Palestinian "casualties" has been researched by history professor Richard Landes (formerly at Boston University and now at Bar Ilan University in Israel), who coined the term "Pallywood" to describe it. Despite the exposure of this trick, the PIDS continue to use it for media manipulation, often finding success with journalists who are gullible at best (and irrevocably biased against Israel at worst). In 2012 Khulood Badawi, a UN employee in Gaza, tweeted a picture of parents holding a dead child, claiming she was killed by an Israeli airstrike, when in fact the picture had been taken in 2009, after she had died in a tragic accident. Later that year, during Israel's Operation Pillar of Defense, BBC reporter Jon Donnison publicized a photo of an alleged Palestinian child victim of Israel's military operations; the photo, which came from a Palestinian journalist in Gaza, was quickly exposed as being a photograph of a Syrian child killed by Bashar Assad's military. In 2018, Basem Naim (a Hamas minister in Gaza) plucked an adorable photograph of an Instagram-famous California toddler from the internet, gave her a made-up Arabic name, and claimed that she was the victim of an Israeli airstrike. Of course, if Israelis and the IDF were

---

[8] http://divestthis.com/2012/06/rhetoric-solutions.html

constantly committing the atrocities they are accused of, why do the PIDS constantly need to fake the evidence? And, you might ask, why do the news media give any credence to their claims? (Once again, filed under "if the Zionists really controlled the media, we wouldn't have this problem.")

We don't need to resort to fraud to talk about Israel's security needs. Almost anyone who has been to Israel has personally been in range of Hamas or Hezbollah rockets. Anyone who has been to Israel knows what it is like to pass through a checkpoint at the entrance to a mall or other public building. We have been to places in which people were killed by suicide bombers. Tell those stories. Make them real to people who are listening.

For example, Gaza is just one mile away from the Israeli town of Sderot, which has been targeted by thousands of missiles. But don't just talk about thousands of missiles; talk instead about four-year-old Yuval Abebah and two-year-old Dorit Benisian, who in 2004 became the first people in Sderot to be murdered by Hamas rocket fire. They were cousins, children of immigrants from Ethiopia. But Hamas rockets don't distinguish between "white" Jews and Jews of color.

I can tell people that, on the day I arrived on my 2003 trip to Israel, I drove right by the Café Hillel in Jerusalem, which had been the target of a suicide bomb attack just three days before. Two of the dead were Dr. David Applebaum, head of emergency medicine at Shaare Zedek Hospital and his daughter Nava, who was to have been married the next day. Instead of a wedding, his family and her fiancé attended their funerals. Dr. Applebaum had treated both Jews and Arabs-- anyone who came into his emergency room was a patient. The suicide terrorist didn't know this, of course. His goal was simply to kill as many Jews as he could.

You can make an anecdote more effective by changing the location from thousands of miles away to your own neighborhood. Pick a spot one mile away and ask how your listener would feel if missiles were being launched at him or her every single day—for years—from the school or apartment building down the street. And then count down from 15 to 0 to let them figure out where they are going to find a shelter in which to watch their life flash before their eyes when the missile explodes nearby. Or pick a location a half a mile away, and ask your listeners to imagine a border with thousands of hostile protestors massed there; some would be armed with firebombs and knives, and they have promised to pull down the border fence, invade your home, and cut out your heart (that was, literally, what Hamas leader Yahya Sinwar threatened they would do to Israelis). That was the scenario along the Gaza border in 2018.

Last but not least, we have The Five Commandments of Successful Advocacy. (Perhaps you were expecting a different, more biblically connected, commandment number? Sorry, I don't want to suggest that these small kernels of advice were the result of any type of divine revelation.)

COMMANDMENT #1: TELL THE TRUTH (OR AT LEAST DON'T KNOWINGLY LIE)

It's important that our side be credible. You won't be able to fact-check on the fly when confronting the PIDS, so it's vital to stick to what you already know is the truth. Of course, this is even more important in any online encounter where your words can remain visible for an eternity. You don't want your rhetorical gaffe about Israel to end up like a drunken party photo posted on Facebook. Even editing a blog post or deleting a Tweet is no protection against the infamous "screen shot" that captures what you initially sent into cyberspace. It should also go without saying that we don't need to resort to "Pallywood" techniques of faked pictures and maliciously edited videos to make our points. And we don't want to find ourselves in the moral sewer inhabited by PIDS who, during Operation Protective Edge in 2014, posted pictures of the murder scene of the Fogel family—butchered in their home by Palestinian terrorists—claiming them to be Gazan victims of IDF operations.

Unfortunately, internet hoaxes exist on our side as well. One famous example was a purported "Letter to An Anti-Zionist Friend" by Dr. Martin Luther King. It reads like a Dr. King speech—but he never wrote it. Its actual origin is unknown. Even the citation of its purported publication (in a magazine called Saturday Review) was in a volume and page that did not correspond to any actual published issues. To help avoid it spreading further, CAMERA (Committee for Accuracy in Middle East Reporting in America, a pro-Israel media watchdog group) published a full exposure of this hoax on its website, so that Israel supporters would know the truth and not continue to cite it. I've never seen any anti-Israel organization show the integrity of doing the same for the multiplicity of faked pictures and quotes that are constantly being circulated on their side; but as their entire arguments are based on falsifying history and facts, that's not a surprise.

You can help ensure the veracity of your information by getting it from established, reliable sources—groups such as StandWithUs, AIPAC, CAMERA, Honest Reporting, American Jewish Committee as well as Israeli government bodies such as the Ministry of Foreign Affairs and the IDF. All of them are very active on social media and are happy to have you disseminate their information.

Also, beyond substance, consider style. Nothing undercuts the punch of an online comment like bad speling and gramur, 'cause if you don't rite good then your statement looks fulish.

COMMANDMENT #2: AVOID AD HOMINEM ATTACKS

The person seeking the moral high ground should also occupy the rhetorical high ground, so never say that the person you're responding to is an idiot. Even when he--or she--is. (For those who remember the original Saturday Night Live "Point-Counterpoint" sketches, avoid the "Jane, you ignorant slut" response.) These people may be wrong on the facts and their train of thought on this issue may not be running at full speed, but they are often otherwise quite functional and rational. Instead, take a deep breath and simply point out the errors of either facts or logic. You can also go "Law and Order" on them and "impeach the witness" if the person (or the organization they represent) has a track record of making statements that are demonstrably wrong.

COMMANDMENT #3: DON'T GENERALIZE

Avoid overly broad statements such as "all Palestinians are supporters of terrorists." Do too many of them support radical Islamist terror? Absolutely—even one is too many. But recognize that just as you want the PIDS to make unforced errors to which you can respond with authority, they want you to do the same. Don't help them out. You can blame the Palestinian leadership for refusing to negotiate peace with

Israel, but you can't blame every Palestinian-in-the-street for that.

COMMANDMENT #4: DON'T DISTORT

Avoid conflating all anti-Israel statements into the most extreme position (which is, for you newbies, supporting Hamas and its calls for genocide). There are ample ways to counter anti-Israel arguments without accusing every Israel boycotter of secretly holding a "Friends of Hamas" membership card. (Though some of them might.)

COMMANDMENT #5: USE POSITIVE LANGUAGE

When confronting the manifold lies of the PIDS about Israel ("apartheid!" "genocide!" "cultural appropriation!" "bad driving!") the temptation is overwhelming to directly respond to them ("Israel is not apartheid!"...though you might be on weak ground about the driving). Studies of human thought and emotional response tell us that this can be counterproductive. The more a lie is repeated, the more believable it becomes. If they say "Israel is committing genocide against the Palestinians" and you say "Israel is not committing genocide!" the words that stick in the listeners mind are the ones that are repeated— "Israel" and "genocide."

You can refute lies using positive statements about Israel. Instead of repeating the claim about Israel and genocide, you can instead say "That's a lie. The Palestinian population in the West Bank and Gaza has more than tripled since 1967." Now try it for the "apartheid" lie. (I'll wait.) Does your response sound something like "The truth is that Israeli Arabs are citizens with equal rights and serve as members of Israel's parliament, Supreme Court, military and foreign service"? Well done! (The

Mossad will be crediting your account with 10 Rothschild points.)

As I will discuss in Chapter Six, the PIDS couch their anti-Israel screeds in the language of "human rights." You should use similarly sympathetic terms that should appeal to your audience. Neil Lazarus suggests that whenever possible, include the words "hope," "peace," "children," and "future" in any statement that you make. As in "Israelis want a future of peace for their children, and also for Palestinian children. We hope that the Palestinian leadership will end its 70-year war against Israel and come to the negotiating table."

A superb example of positive and inspiring language is found in a short video from StandWithUs entitled "If You Will It, It Is No Dream": "Over 3000 years ago, an indigenous people developed a thriving civilization and culture in their ancestral homeland. Over time they were conquered by a series of aggressive foreign empires. While some stayed in their own communities, most of them gradually scattered across Europe and the Middle East. For 1900 years they lived as a mostly oppressed stateless minority, suffering persecution, expulsions and ultimately genocide. They barely survived but never lost hope of returning to their homeland. Once released from their ghettoes, they started a liberation movement and went home to join those who were already there. And they built one of the most vibrant, diverse, inspiring nations the world has ever seen. That nation is the state of the Jewish people—Israel."
(It's even better with the visuals and the music—check it out at https://www.youtube.com/watch?v=cuiKSH-jUYY.)

The public opinion pollster Frank Luntz, who works with several Israel advocacy groups, conducted a poll in July 2015 in which he pointed out several positive messages that resonated widely among audiences, even left-leaning audiences that have developed a bizarre sympathy for Islamist terrorists who preach religious hatred and even oppress their own women. They are:

• "Everyone in Israel is free to practice their religion and worship their God. No other Middle Eastern country offers similar religious protections."

• "Women in Israel have exactly the same rights as men. No other Middle Eastern country offers women fully equal rights."

• "Despite the ongoing conflict with Gaza, Israel still facilitates the donation of tens of millions in humanitarian aid to Palestinians and opens its hospitals to treat them."

All of these are true, and opinion polling tells us that these messages work—so use them!

Now that you have some tools to work with, let's go meet our less-than-friendly neighborhood PIDS.

Key Points:

The Jewish people have just as much right as anyone else to national self-determination.

Israeli and American policy supports two states for two peoples—the PIDS will oppose this.

Use ARM, use positive language, and use anecdotes that make the situation real.

Chapter 4: A Field Guide to PIDS

Politics makes strange bedfellows. – Charles Dudley Warner, American essayist and novelist.

It's not hard to find people who hate Israel, especially if you live in certain geographic areas. The Reut Institute in Tel Aviv has identified five "hubs of delegitimization" of Israel in the world. These locales are places where various networks of PIDS operate together: Madrid, Brussels, London, Toronto and my own home, the San Francisco Bay Area. In any of these cities, you'll find most types of PIDS well represented. If you live in places like Dallas or Miami Beach, where the natural habitats of PIDS – far leftist coffee shops and bookstores –are less common, you'll have to look harder for them. If you haven't seen these types before – or if you have, but you're uncertain how and why they got to be the way they are – fear not. Here's a handy-dandy breakdown of all the species of PIDS. They will vary in their plumage and their warblings, but they're all infected with the same strain of Israel-hating extremism.

THE EXTREME LEFT

Photo courtesy of zombie of zombietime.com

Usual habitat: non-corporate coffee shops and bookstores, especially those featuring Marxist logos. These are hot spots for planning public "peace" rallies to support "revolutionary" wars across the world. The protests are often followed by "spontaneous" street rioting.

Political leaning: the Green Party is far too conservative for them.

Role Models: North Korea, and Soviet dictator Josef Stalin.

Reading: *Counterpunch*, the favorite magazine of the extreme left, which publishes articles such as "Pol Pot Revisited"--which denied the Cambodian genocide-- and "North Korea's Justifiable Anger," alongside pieces claiming that Israel steals organs for transplantation from dead Palestinians. Also, Das Kapital (the seminal work on political economics by Karl Marx).

Identifying marks: Che Guevara T shirts.

Their call: "We are not just for peace, we are for the victory of the resistance!" (Richard Becker, West Coast Director of ANSWER Coalition, at a November 2008 rally in San Francisco.)

Strange bedfellows: 9-11 truthers, Islamist groups and far right-wing anti-Semites.

THE AGING HIPPIES

Photo courtesy of zombie of zombietime.com

-Usual habitat: the letters page of your local newspaper, anti-Israel lectures in libraries, streetcorner vigils, and food co-op boycott rallies.

Political leaning: "progressive."

Role models: Themselves... in 1969.

Reading: Noam Chomsky, the Jewish radical MIT professor (not of international relations or political science, but rather of linguistics, which somehow makes him an expert on the Middle East. In addition to being anti-Zionist, Chomsky claimed in 2013 that President Obama "is running the biggest terrorist operation that exists, maybe in history.")

Identifying marks: Birkenstocks.

Their call: "No Justice. No Peace."

Strange bedfellows: Ron Paul supporters.

THE YOUNG "FAUX-GRESSIVES"

Usual habitat: Progressive Democrats of America, panel discussions purporting to explain how anti-Zionism isn't anti-Semitism, and any unrelated event that they can hijack to the "Palestinian cause."

Political leaning: Bernie Sanders. Because anyone to the right of Bernie is really a Republican.

Role model: Linda Sarsour, the Women's March leader who demands that Zionists be excluded from social justice movements.

Reading: *Daily Kos* and *ZNet*, online platforms that provide regular doses of articles by prominent PIDS.

Identifying marks: Wokeness.

Their call: "Nothing is creepier than Zionism." (Sarsour)

Strange bedfellow: Louis Farrakhan (aka "Black David Duke"), whose old-school anti-Semitism, homophobia, misogyny and race-baiting are not a problem for Sarsour and her fellow Women's March leaders Carmen Perez and Tamika Mallory (who is proud to attend events and be photographed with Farrakhan, who she calls the "Greatest of All Time").

(For my friends in the UK: your answers to the above are—in order-- Momentum, Jeremy Corbyn, Lauren Booth, *The Guardian*, the Labour red rose, "Oh, Jeremy Corbyn," and any of the radical Islamists in the UK who echo Farrakhan's hate speech.)

THE CHRISTIAN "PEACEMAKERS"

http://lumpygrumpyandfrumpy.blogspot.com/2010/0
1/torontos- no-go-zones-for-zionists.html

Usual habitat: Churches, "peace" missions to the West
Bank, and interfaith dialogues with anti-Israel Jews.

Political leaning: Earnestly liberal.

Role models: Naim Ateek, founder of the Christian Arab
organization Sabeel. Sabeel's rhetoric uses crucifixion analogies
against Israel, and claims that Judaism has been superseded by
Christianity so is therefore is no longer a valid religion (a
philosophy abandoned years ago by most American churches).

Reading: Walt and Mearsheimer's The Israel Lobby and
US Foreign Policy. Published in 2007, this best-selling book by
two academics claims that efforts by American citizens to
encourage a pro-Israel American policy are harmful to the
interests of the United States. It was met with widespread
criticism that it was based on sloppy scholarship and selective

use of history, such as completely ignoring Palestinian terrorism and its role in shaping American public opinion.

Identifying marks: Basic black clothing, head to toe.

Their call: None, as they are usually conducting a silent vigil.

Strange bedfellows: Radical Islamist preachers whose agenda is "first the Saturday people, then the Sunday people."

THE ISLAMIST YOUTH

Photo courtesy of zombie of zombietime.com

Usual habitat: Universities and street protests.

Political leaning: The Hamas charter, which says: "There is no solution for the Palestinian question except through Jihad. Initiatives, proposals and international conferences are all a waste of time and vain endeavors."

Role models: Palestinian rioters who throw rocks at Israeli civilian cars.

Reading: Ali Abunimah, Palestinian-American activist who wrote <u>One Country: A Bold Proposal to End the Israeli-Palestinian Conflict</u>, which proposes eliminating the Jewish state of Israel entirely. (More on this "one-state final solution" in Chapter Seven, and more on Abunimah in Chapter Eleven).

Identifying marks: Keffiyehs, and T-shirts or flags with bloody fists.

Their call: "From the river to the sea, Palestine will be free."

Strange bedfellows: LGBT PIDS (which is very strange given the extreme repression of LGBT individuals in Arab countries, not to mention Iran's frequent public hangings of gays – despite former Iranian president Mahmoud Ahmedinejad's odd claim they don't exist there).

THE OLD SCHOOL ANTI-SEMITES

Photo courtesy of zombie of zombietime.com

Usual habitat: Any gathering of the above groups, trying to blend in.

Political leaning: Politics? It's all part of the "Jewish conspiracy" that is responsible for both capitalism and Communism.

Role model: Hitler.

Reading: What else? Mein Kampf.

Their call: "F#&@! the Jews."

Identifying marks: Signs with openly anti-Semitic phrases such as "Smash the Jewish State."

Strange bedfellows: Any human beings that will tolerate them.

THE EXTREME RIGHT

Former Ku Klux Klan Grand Wizard David Duke

(source: Emmanuel d'Aubignosc, Wikimedia Commons)

Usual habitat: Out in the mountains, hiding from the United Nations black helicopters that are coming to take away our freedoms.

Political leaning: So far right that they meet up with the extreme left wing well beyond the boundaries of reasonable political discourse.

Role model: Former Ku Klux Klan Grand Wizard and Louisiana politician David Duke, who has stated that "Judaism at its core... is a racist religion."[9]

Reading: Alison Weir – not the esteemed British historian of the Tudor era, but rather the online peddler of misinformation via her "If Americans Knew" website. She refers to suicide bombers as "freedom fighters" and has wrongly claimed that there was an independent Arab country of Palestine prior to the creation of the State of Israel.

Their call: "It's the International Jewish Conspiracy."

Identifying marks: Often none, which allows them to pass as normal people.

Strange bedfellow: Cynthia McKinney, extreme-left former Democratic Congresswoman who was best known in Congress for physically attacking a US Capitol police officer.

---

[9] http://www.zionism-israel.com/news/duke_anti_zionism.htm

And finally, THE ANTI-ZIONIST JEWS

Source: Wikimedia Commons

Usual habitat: San Francisco, Seattle, and universities in which they are enrolled in their eighth year of two-year graduate degree programs in "peace and conflict studies" or "gender identity theory."

Political leaning: Whoever is the most anti-Israel candidate in any given election.

Role model: The contrary child from the "four children" parable in the Passover Haggadah.

Identifying marks: Asymmetrical hairstyles and piercings in painful places.

Their call: "Not in our name" followed by something incomprehensible regarding "privilege" and "oppression."

Reading: Ilan Pappé's <u>The Ethnic Cleansing of Palestine</u> and Max Blumenthal's <u>Goliath</u>. Pappé is a Marxist ex-Israeli who claims that Israel deliberately expelled Palestinians en masse in 1947-8 and who admits that his work is influenced more by ideology than by historical fact. Blumenthal's book allegedly provides deep insights into the racism of Israeli society despite the fact that he can't even read Hebrew. <u>Goliath</u> was so far removed from any semblance of reality that Eric Alterman (who has himself been highly critical of Israel's policies towards the Palestinians), writing in the far left magazine *The Nation*, termed it "The I Hate Israel Handbook." He bitingly noted that "this book could have been published by the Hamas Book-of-the-Month Club (if it existed) without a single word change once it's translated into Arabic."[10]

(We'll meet Pappé and Blumenthal again in Chapter Eleven.)

Strange bedfellows: Neturei Karta, the ultra-Orthodox anti-Zionist sect which opposes any Jewish sovereignty in the land of Israel until the return of the Messiah. They're such an authentic example of traditional Judaism that their history goes all the way back to.... 1938. It's quite a bizarre spectacle when these men in their black hats and beards stand alongside secular fringe group anti-Israel demonstrators outside major pro-Israel events, just as when they stood alongside former PLO chief

---

[10] http://www.thenation.com/blog/176723/israel-haters-handbook-continued

Yasser Arafat and former Iranian President Mahmoud Ahmedinejad.

All of these groups of PIDS loudly promote the myth that criticism of Israel within the United States is in some way "muzzled." If only we lived in a nation where PIDS could march openly in our streets with Hezbollah and Hamas flags. If only we lived in a society where a sloppily written screed like Walt and Mearsheimer's <u>The Israel Lobby</u> became a nationwide bestseller. If only we lived in a country where PIDS could disrupt speeches or cultural performances by Israelis, or even forcibly take over the dais at national convocations of church groups which declined to adopt hard-line anti-Israel positions. If only our universities were places where professors could, without any consequence, mock pro-Israel students in class and use public resources to spread lies and hate speech about Israel, and were able to offer their facilities for meetings of anti-Israel organizations. If only major newspapers such as the *Washington Post, New York Times, Los Angeles Times* and *The Wall Street Journal* ran Op-Ed pieces from leading anti-Israel figures (and sometimes even from Hamas leaders themselves) while their reporters on the ground in Gaza refuse to report on Hamas' use of hospitals and schools for firing rockets. If only major online sites such as *DailyKos* and *HuffingtonPost* repeatedly featured articles written by PIDS. Ah, then we'd have open conversation in this country about Israel!

Of course, all of these things do happen—all too frequently. So when looking at the wide and deep support for Israel among the American public, why have the PIDS simply been unable to generate such support for their side? The reason is simply that the "Palestinian narrative" just fails to get traction, once people are aware of the truth. The Palestinians do have a narrative, but the Jewish people have history.

Key Points:

Gatherings of PIDS can be a mix of diverse groups.

These groups often agree on nothing else besides their hatred of Israel. (But "priorities", right?)

Chapter 5: A Palestinese Lexicon

If thought can corrupt language, language can also corrupt thought. - George Orwell, 1984.

Just as you can't tell the players without a scorecard, it's also important to understand the language used by PIDS, because their terminology doesn't necessarily match the conventional meanings of the words they use.

Philippe Assouline, who has written in *The Times of Israel* and has appeared on both American and Israeli television news programs as a commentator, has created a satirical "Palestinese Lexicon"[11] to help unlock this code. Here are some lightly edited samples from the Lexicon:

---

[11] http://blogs.timesofisrael.com/a-palestinese-lexicon/

Aboriginal/Native: Any non-Jew, preferably Arab, whose family has immigrated to Israel/Palestine within the last 150 years or is a remnant of Arab colonial conquests. For example, Yasser Arafat, who was born in Egypt, is a "Native" Palestinian.

Apartheid: The only system in the Middle East which is democratic and grants all Arab citizens full equality under the law, including the right to become a Justice of the Supreme Court, an ambassador, a military officer or a Minister in the Cabinet., i.e. a form of "Racism" specific to Israel. Not to be confused with the widespread discrimination against Palestinians on ethnic grounds in Lebanon, which is not Apartheid.

Apartheid Wall: A separation fence erected in response to countless terror attacks in order to protect both Jews and Muslims from suicide bombings as a manifestation of Zionist Aggression.

Checkpoint: An absolutely gratuitous, cruel and malicious security measure erected by Israel in the West Bank in response to years of deadly suicide bombings, to be equated with the worst forms of human torture. Not to be confused with security checkpoints at airports and international borders which, though identical in the inconveniences they cause, are perfectly acceptable.

Civilian: An armed Palestinian terrorist in the act of planning or staging a terror attack who is targeted or killed by Israel.

Ethnic Cleansing: The process by which Israel offered Arab people citizenship despite a genocidal war waged by Arab leaders in 1948, and which has given its Arab citizens full democratic rights and enabled its Arab population to thrive and grow at a rate faster than the Jewish majority. e.g., The sprawling Israeli-Arab town of Umm al Fahm is proof of Ethnic Cleansing by Israel.

Equal Rights: "Rights" that are to be acquired for Palestinians, by violence if necessary, and denied to Jews.

Flotilla: A 2010 assemblage of ships carrying expired medications and damaged medical equipment from Turkey to Gaza. The ships carried 400 armed Turkish Jihadis singing about their dream of "Martyrdom" and four confused, elderly "Jewish" women who thought they were on a cruise to Fort Lauderdale. Also, known as a Human Rights stunt.

Frustration: Murderous anti-Semitism that directly precedes Resistance.

Genocide: The deliberate campaign by Zionists to exterminate Palestinian Arabs, which has resulted in the explosion of the Palestinian population from between 600,000 and 700,000 in 1948 to over six million today, including over one million Israeli Palestinians represented in the Israeli parliament.

History: Whatever set of changing fictions is needed to promote the present set of Palestinian claims.

Holocaust: The excessively documented (albeit entirely fabricated) industrial mass murder of European Jewry that was aided by Palestinian nationalist leader Haj Amin al-Husseini but never happened. Also, the current plight of Palestinians.

Human Rights: The religiously uncritical devotion to Palestinian narratives that misuses language associated with the Holocaust in order to demonize the Jewish state and prevent people in real need throughout the world from getting the attention or redress that they deserve. Also, the political philosophy that is not applicable to Arab states and aims to criticize only America and Israel. E.g., "Human Rights prevent me as an NGO head from paying attention to genocide in the Congo lest disapproval of Israel abate temporarily."

Jerusalem: An Occupied Arab capital and central focal point of Arab culture and aspirations for 3,000 years, despite the fact that — unlike Cordoba, Baghdad, Damascus, Mecca, Cairo, Timbuktu or Dearborn, Michigan — it was never an Arab capital or central focal point of Arab culture. Also, an area absolutely bereft of any significance to Jewish people or Jewish history. See also Bethlehem, Rachel's Tomb, Hebron, Shiloh and the Brown Derby Deli.

Jews: A group descended from the Khazar Turkic people who have no connection whatsoever to the ancient Judeans or Israelites who were in fact "Palestinians." Also refers to the group of people who supply Palestinian propagandists with theories, mouthpieces and arguments. e.g. Noam Chomsky is a Jew; Israeli Prime Minister Benjamin Netanyahu is not a Jew.

Judaism: An abstract concept of liberal, pro-Palestinian ethics that is no way tied to 3,500 years of Jewish history on the land of Israel. Not to be confused with the religion of Jesus or the Prophets who were, of course, Palestinian.

Judea: A made up political term for the territory known since classical antiquity as "the West Bank."

Justice: The immediate and unquestioning surrender to every perpetually expanding Palestinian demand, however unreasonable, baseless or insulting.

Martyr: Any person who dies while killing or attempting to kill Zionist civilians having a picnic.

Massacre: Any death of one or more Palestinian terrorists in an armed fight usually started by said terrorists (these include, but are not limited to, those that are imagined or real, or accidental or deliberate). Also, every act of Jewish self-defense...ever. Usually found in a string of terms given as an answer by PLO spokesman Saeb Erekat to any question by a reporter (even those on Entertainment Tonight), i.e., "...struggle, checkpoint, massacre, guns breed guns, bullets breed bullets.... Angelina Jolie has lost too much weight because of the Occupation."

Occupation: The perpetual state of Palestinian affairs, regardless of the total absence of Israeli soldiers in certain Palestinian areas, and an excuse for every single Palestinian excess, including public domestic violence and high cholesterol. Unsaid, is that this political affliction is characterized by the fact that 96% of Palestinians are governed by their own elected leaders.

Occupied: The state of any geographic area populated by Zionists, preferably an area with a long, undisputed Jewish history. e.g. The Western Wall and Temple Mount in "Jerusalem" are Occupied; The Ramat Aviv Gimmel neighborhood of Tel Aviv is Occupied. Also, the perpetual state of the Gaza strip which has not a single "Zionist" in it.

Oppression: Jewish self-determination and any reminders thereof. e.g. A border control between Gaza and Israel is Oppression. Also, anything that a Palestinian activist doesn't like. e.g. "Hamas losing the war it caused in 2009 is a form of Oppression."

Palestinian: A European construct that is shorthand for the eternal victim and a symbol for every sexy cause and/or Hollywood hero. Other usages: a convenient object of self-serving and Narcissistic far-leftist pity; summer "Activism" internships; and the expiating of Holocaust guilt. Not to be confused with...see below.

Palestinian: A Palestinese term for an ancient Arabic people that suddenly materialized in the twentieth century but counts among its members patriotic Jews living on the land of Israel millennia ago. e.g. Jesus, a Judean Rabbi, was a Palestinian. Also used for objects: the Dead Sea Scrolls are Palestinian artifacts.

Palestinian State: A geographic and political entity that is to live side by side as well as over and instead of the Zionist Entity. Also, the answer to all of life's ills, including international terrorism and ring around the collar.

Palestinian Statelessness: Even if not entirely true, the most urgent and pressing issue ... in the history of mankind. Though the direct result of Arab refusal to accept the UN partition plan and the rejection of every subsequent Israeli peace offer, it is entirely the product of Zionist Aggression. Was somehow irrelevant from 1948 to 1967 when Jordan occupied the "West Bank" and Egypt occupied Gaza.

Peace: The process by which Israel voluntarily ethnically cleanses every last Jewish person from territory with deep Jewish significance that it won in a defensive war, in exchange for increased terrorism, demonization, European and Turkish meddling and summits at the White House.

Peace Activist: Alternatively, Turkish Jihadists known for supporting Al Qaeda or misguided Westerners to be used as fig leaves for Jihad.

Peoplehood: The state of every grouping of individuals that share a history, language, culture and geographic origin, except when they are Jewish.

Propaganda: Any documented historical fact that supports the Zionist perspective.

Racism: Any expression of Jewish will that is not a parroting of Palestinian claims. e.g. It is Racism to insist on teaching the Holocaust.

Racist: The state of any act, event, person or thing that accepts in any way, tacit or explicit, the existence of Israel or interrupts, albeit temporarily, the world's obsessive preoccupation with Palestinians' claims. E.g. "A moment of silence to commemorate the loss of athletes murdered by PLO terrorists in 1972 is Racist;" "Cherry tomatoes are Racist." Also, an adjective which is always appropriate before any word, whether referring to an object, abstract concept, medical device or person who is related to Zionists. e.g. "The Racist pill-cam that saved my mother-in-law's life was made in the Zionist Entity by War Criminals."

Real Jew: Any person with a long, Eastern European-sounding family name (ideally ending with 'Y') who is also vocally anti-Zionist. e.g., "Although the Holocaust is a fiction stemming from Zionist Aggression, Kapos were Real Jews.

Refugee: Any Arab anywhere in the world who claims that one of his relatives was forced to leave Israel as a result of the war started by Arabs to prevent the state of Israel from being established. Jews who were expelled from Arab states in 1948 as a result of the same war are not to be included in this term.

Resistance: The act of deliberately murdering (unarmed) Israeli school children or other innocents in restaurants, buses, nurseries or other areas or the firing of rockets at elderly people without provocation. e.g. "Massacring 11 Israeli athletes who were napping in their rooms at the Munich Olympics was Resistance."

Right: Any Palestinian demand. This term does not apply to Jews.

Starvation/Humanitarian Catastrophe: With respect to Gaza, the state of having food and all necessary supplies provided by Israeli deliveries, allowing the opening of malls, water parks and luxury hotels.

State of Israel: A Racist term for the Zionist Entity.

Terrorism: Attacks on Egyptian soldiers by Palestinians; when suffered by Zionists, a fictitious and Racist concept.

War Crimes: Any historically documented act of Israeli non-aggression. E.g. "The transforming by Zionists of desert lands into watermelon patches is a War Crime."

War Criminal: Any Zionist who is about to get airtime or give a speech at UC Berkeley or Montreal's Concordia University. E.g. "Israel's top fashion model Bar Rafaeli is a War Criminal."

Western Wall: An appendage to the Haram el Sharif in Jerusalem, with no significance to Jews – though it was the Prophet Mohammed's parking spot for his flying horse al Buraq.

Zionism: The inchoate and indefinable global movement for evil that is the cause of all ills plaguing the Arab world since 1300 AD (the Arab world includes Mauritania, Yemen and Malmo, Sweden), as well as the cause of the meltdown of the Western financial system. Expressed by such pernicious phenomena as the credit crisis of 2008, slow Syrian internet connections and trained sharks operating as spies off of the Egyptian coast.

Zionist: A catch-all umbrella term for all villains everywhere, throughout history, in any field of human endeavor, even if they actively opposed Zionism, E.g. Hitler was a "Zionist" although he did nothing wrong because the "Holocaust" never happened, although it is happening to Palestinians today. Also, synonym of Jew (and not in a good way). The following people have all been accused of being "Zionist" by their political opponents: deposed Egyptian President Mohammed Morsi, deposed Libyan leader Muammar Ghadafi, Syrian President Bashar al-Assad, former Iranian President Mahmoud Ahmedinejad, former al Qaeda leader Osama bin Laden, and Hezbollah leader Hassan Nasrallah.

Zionist Aggression: The response, after ample warning, to unprovoked Resistance against unarmed women and children and/or any act of self-defense when carried out by Jews. E.g. "It was Zionist Aggression that the Israel police officer shot a Palestinian terrorist attempting to run over cars full of Israelis with his bulldozer."

Zionist Entity: A colonial, illegitimate and evil collection of people who, as a form of Propaganda and Racism, regularly produce scientific breakthroughs and supermodels that alleviate human suffering and improve life everywhere.

Key point:

PIDS have definitions of key concepts such as "apartheid," "Zionism" and "racism" which don't match the actual meanings of those terms.

Chapter 6: They've Got Issues, We've Got Answers

A half-truth is the most cowardly of lies. –Mark Twain

When attacking Israel, PIDS focus on misinforming the public about three main issues, occupation (including settlements), refugees and human rights. PIDS will exploit all of these issues as different roads to the same destination: not just an attack on Israel's policies or behavior, but a challenge to its very legitimacy as a nation-state.

Criticism of Israel's handling of these issues doesn't necessarily delegitimize it; anyone who reads the Israeli press knows that patriotic Israelis will indeed criticize their government, and often quite vigorously. That's the price of freedom and of the use of state power, neither of which Jews had for centuries.[12]

Part of the consequence of having state power is the power to make mistakes, and the responsibility for dealing with such mistakes. Even the most partisan supporter of Israel should not attempt to claim that Israel has been perfect in its handling of the many challenges it has faced. But the PIDS will routinely bring up mistakes made by Israel or the pre-state Zionists, such as the massacre at Deir Yassin by the Irgun militia in 1948 (see Chapter Two), as reasons why Israel shouldn't exist. But the logical conclusion of "Deir Yassin happened...." is not "therefore Israel is an illegitimate state and should cease to exist."

Yet while the PIDS want to hold Israel to an unreasonable standard of perfection, they excuse any Palestinian misconduct as being the result of "occupation." This is actually a subtle form of racism, the soft bigotry of low expectations—claiming that the Palestinians cannot be expected to behave in accord with "Western" standards of morality (such as not conducting suicide bombings in pizza parlors, not slitting the throats of babies sleeping in their cribs, and not using mass media to incite religious hatred). "Occupation" and "oppression" are given as excuses for mass murders of Israeli civilians, while any action by Israel that harms a single Palestinian is breathlessly

---

[12] Some of the most interesting and challenging discussions about the use of such power—and how Jewish teachings can guide it-- are held under the auspices of the Shalom Hartman Institute in Jerusalem and are available in English in blogs and videos on their website http://hartmaninstitute.com/.

trumpeted by PIDS as evidence that Israel's very existence is illegitimate.

Along the same lines, PIDS will use any evidence of inequality between Israel's Jewish and Arab populations as proof of an irredeemable "racism" that can only be ended by the elimination of the Jewish state.

You can effectively respond to these issues—as long as you know the key facts.

Occupation: Are They Talking About 1967? Or 1948?

The first response to anyone talking about Israel's occupation is to ask them to define their use of the term. Let's acknowledge that about 150,000 Arabs living in area C of the West Bank are governed under the international laws of military occupation. (Area C, comprising about 60% of the land area across the Green Line, is under full Israeli political and security control under terms of the 1995 "Oslo II" agreement between Israel and the PA. Only 5% of the Arab population across the Green Line, not counting Jerusalem, lives in Area C. The other 95% live under the rule of the Palestinian Authority.) Even former Israeli Prime Minister Ariel Sharon used the word "kibush," Hebrew for "occupation." Although Israel has not annexed any of the settlement blocs in Area C, I'm not suggesting that Israel is morally wrong to stay there in absence of a genuine peace agreement.

This question—"exactly what territory are you describing as 'occupied'?"-- must be asked to sort out those people who openly declare their membership in the PIDS by talking about the "occupation" as if it started in 1948. In their Israel-hating minds, Tel Aviv and Haifa (which have been part of

Israel since 1948) are just as much "occupied Arab lands" as the city of Ariel in Samaria. Note the "60 years" reference on this T-shirt from 2008:

"...because 60 years is a long ass time to be under occupation!"

photo courtesy of Eclectic Infidel

Now you already know the response to these folks (if not, go back to Chapter Three): "So, just to be clear, you oppose peace between a Jewish state of Israel and an Arab state of Palestine? And unless Israel decides to commit national suicide, you're going to support ongoing action to destroy it?" As anyone who has tried to engage with these people knows, they can't help admitting it. At which point anyone listening who shares the position of the overwhelming majority of Americans-- support for Israel's right to live in peace, free from attacks and threats of destruction-- has already decided on which side of this discussion they are standing.

Objecting to Israel's military and civilian presence in Judea and Samaria is different than declaring all of Israel to be "occupied Arab lands." Not everyone who holds that position is an Israel-hater, but you should know the facts when this issue is raised. To begin with, this is not territory that "belongs" to any currently existing country. It was part of the British Mandate, and the United Nations had recommended that it be part of a Palestinian Arab state. King Abdullah of Jordan had other ideas, and in 1950 annexed it to his kingdom (in a step that created absolutely no international hysteria). The UN remained strangely quiet and did not issue a single condemnation of Jordan for its actions. Given that no country holds valid legal title to this land, some people prefer to use the term "disputed territories." The status of this area is somewhat different than, for example, the Turkish occupation of the northern half of the actual country of Cyprus, which has not generated even a miniscule fraction of the attention that the UN has devoted to Israel. (Wait, you didn't know about that one either? It started in 1974, and Turkey even set up a puppet Turkish regime in northern Cyprus recognized only by Turkey itself.)

The PIDS would also like you to forget how the IDF took over this area in June 1967. As you recall from the timeline in Chapter Two, the Arab states massed their armies on Israel's borders and openly declared that their goal was the elimination of the Jewish state. King Hussein of Jordan, despite appeals from Israel transmitted to him by UN officials, chose to initiate hostilities against Israel by shelling civilians in Jerusalem. Israel responded militarily to end the threat to its capital and its eastern border (which was, at its narrowest point, only nine miles away from the Mediterranean). That's how the Jordanian occupation ended.

It's also important to note that, despite the recurrent references to "international law," Israel's presence in Judea and Samaria is not "illegal." The most definitive statement on this is United Nations Resolution 242, passed unanimously by the Security Council in November of 1967.

Here's the text:

"The Security Council,

Expressing its continuing concern with the grave situation in the Middle East,

Emphasizing the inadmissibility of the acquisition of territory by war and the need to work for a just and lasting peace in which every State in the area can live in security,

Emphasizing further that all Member States in their acceptance of the Charter of the United Nations have undertaken a commitment to act in accordance with Article 2 of the Charter,

Affirms that the fulfillment of Charter principles requires the establishment of a just and lasting peace in the Middle East which should include the application of both the following principles:

Withdrawal of Israeli armed forces from territories occupied in the recent conflict;

Termination of all claims or states of belligerency and respect for and acknowledgement of the sovereignty, territorial integrity and political independence of every State in the area and their right to live in peace within secure and recognized boundaries free from threats or acts of force;

Affirms further the necessity

For guaranteeing freedom of navigation through international waterways in the area;

For achieving a just settlement of the refugee problem;

For guaranteeing the territorial inviolability and political independence of every State in the area, through measures including the establishment of demilitarized zones;

Requests the Secretary General to designate a Special Representative to proceed to the Middle East to establish and maintain contacts with the States concerned in order to promote agreement and assist efforts to achieve a peaceful and accepted settlement in accordance with the provisions and principles in this resolution;

Requests the Secretary-General to report to the Security Council on the progress of the efforts of the Special Representative as soon as possible."

When reading this text, several points are noteworthy. The first is the enshrinement of the "land for peace" formula, while noting that withdrawal from lands conquered by Israel must be accompanied by peace (rather than the Arab League formulation of "withdraw first, then we can talk about peaceful relations" or the Hamas version which is "withdraw first, then maybe we'll think about a temporary truce until we are stronger.")

The second is the absence of certain key words. Note that the words "all" or "the" do not appear before the word "territories." This was not an oversight. The two main drafters of the resolution were the United Kingdom's Lord Caradon and the American Arthur Goldberg. Lord Caradon wrote: "I would defend absolutely what we did. It was not for us to lay down exactly where the border should be. I know the 1967 border very well. It is not a satisfactory border, it is where troops had to stop in 1948, just where they happened to be that night, that is not a permanent boundary." And Goldberg clearly noted: "Does Resolution 242 as unanimously adopted by the UN Security Council require the withdrawal of Israeli armed forces from all of the territories occupied by Israel during the 1967 war? The answer is no. In the resolution, the words 'the' and 'all' are omitted. Resolution 242 calls for the withdrawal of Israeli armed forces from territories occupied in the 1967 conflict, without specifying the extent of the withdrawal. The resolution, therefore, neither commands nor prohibits total withdrawal. If the resolution is ambiguous, and purposely so, on this crucial issue, how is the withdrawal issue to be settled? By direct negotiations between the concerned parties. Resolution 242 calls for agreement between them to achieve a peaceful and accepted settlement. Agreement and acceptance necessarily require negotiations."[13]

Funny how that word "negotiations" keeps popping up. And while there have been intermittent negotiations, the Palestinian leadership—and the PIDS in the West—prefer to bypass this essential ingredient of peacemaking, instead calling upon the United States, the European Union and the international community to take coercive action against Israel.

---

[13] http://www.camera.org/index.asp?x_context=2&x_outlet=118&x_article=1267

The past four Prime Ministers of Israel have all called for an end to Israel's presence in much of Judea and Samaria, and Ariel Sharon withdrew all Israelis from Gaza in 2005—an experience that resulted in incessant rocket fire from that area, especially after Hamas took power in the 2007 coup. Rockets from Gaza led to Israel's three major actions in response, Operation Cast Lead in 2008, Operation Pillar of Defense in 2012 and Operation Protective Edge in 2014. So Israel is not about to repeat that experience and bring its population centers, capital and international airport within range of potential short range rocket fire from the West Bank—not without the Palestinian leadership openly declaring in Arabic, to its own people, peace with Israel, and not without some mechanism guaranteeing Israel's security. Whether such a development is even possible in the near future is certainly subject to debate. But this issue, like the others separating Israel and the Palestinian leadership, can only be resolved by negotiation.

Settlements are part of the discussion about occupation. Yet within the pro-Israel community, there is a range of opinions about the civilian settlements. Not all settlements are alike. Some, such as the Gush Etzion region, south of Jerusalem, are in locations from which Jews were ethnically cleansed in 1948. Some, like Ariel and Ma'aleh Adumim, are small cities built in previously undeveloped open space. Hebron has a small area of Jewish residences in a city that had unbroken Jewish presence for centuries until it was ethnically cleansed in 1929; Jews returned there in 1968. Other settlements are just a few trailers on a remote hilltop.

Are the settlements an obstacle to peace? Yes-- because Israel and the Palestinians disagree about them, as they do about a host of other issues: refugees, incitement, and water rights, just to name a few. There's no need to deny that fact.

Though you might also ask why an area that was Jew-free for a period of only 19 years (the Old City of Jerusalem), or even 40 years (Hebron) must remain Jew-free forever.

Are the settlements **the** obstacle to peace, or even the main obstacle? Of course not. You can prove that by asking any of the PIDS a slightly different version of the key question: "If Israel were to withdraw from every settlement beyond the June 4 1967 armistice line tomorrow, and allow the creation of a Jew-free state of Palestine, would you then support Israel's right to live in peace as the state of the Jewish people?" And, of course, they will answer "no." Because their diatribes against Israel's presence in Judea and Samaria are only their starting point. It's the starter drug—cheap, easily available, more socially acceptable—before they introduce the more toxic stuff that they are peddling.

The PIDS will always lead with the issue of the settlements, but that's not the ground on which you want to have a discussion. As the Chinese writer Sun Tzu wrote in his classic The Art of War, "the way is to avoid what is strong and to strike at what is weak." Regardless of your own opinions on settlements, the consistent public position of the American government has been to oppose settlement activity, and many patriotic Israelis oppose settlements as well. So debating PIDS solely on the issue of settlements allows them to talk from a position of strength, and to hide their actual agenda: eliminating Tel Aviv, which they also consider to be an "illegal settlement." Don't let them do it. Instead, use ARM to move the discussion to the core issue: "Yes, the settlements are a controversial issue, along with many others that separate Israelis and Palestinians. But that's not the root of the conflict. The root of the conflict is the failure of the Palestinian leadership to accept living in peace alongside a Jewish state of Israel regardless of where the borders are. I hope the Palestinians will accept that. Then negotiations can solve all of the other issues and lead to a future of peace for both Palestinian and Israeli children." (We'll get to the details of the alternative proposed by the PIDS, the fallacious "one-state solution," in Chapter Seven.)

Refugees: A Demographic Weapon Aimed at Israel's Existence

The Palestinian refugee issue is at the core of the Israeli-Palestinian conflict. It was created by the Arab refusal to accept a Jewish state in the Jewish homeland, it was perpetuated by the Arabs as a political weapon against Israel, and it is the excuse currently given by the Palestinians for their ongoing rejection of peace with the Jewish state.

The refugees are the key ongoing issue in what the PIDS regard as the original sin of the establishment of Israel. In their narrative, the Western nations, through the United Nations, took Palestine from its indigenous Arab inhabitants (who were just minding their own business and peacefully coexisting with the Jews) and gave it away to a group of European Jewish colonizers as compensation for the Holocaust. Not only does this perverted account ignore thirty centuries of Jewish history in the Jewish homeland, most of it prior to the arrival of the Arab imperial conquest, but it also—deliberately—overlooks the achievements of the Zionist movement in building the foundations of the state decades before the Holocaust. It also dismisses the heavy price paid by the Jews to successfully defend their newborn state. By presenting Israel's legitimacy as being dependent on the Holocaust, it also encourages the type of Holocaust denial promoted by Iran and by anti-Israel activists in the West. UK Labour party members were recently exposed to be spreading Holocaust denial and other classic anti-Semitic tropes in multiple "pro-Palestinian" Facebook groups, some of which included Labour leader Jeremy Corbyn as an active member.

There are very few facts that are not in dispute about the refugees. About the only details that are agreed upon are that within the area proposed by the United Nations for a Jewish state in 1947, there were about 400,000 Arabs; and by the end of Israel's War of Independence, there were about 159,000 Arabs remaining within the newly expanded borders of the state (which encompassed significant territory that had originally been designated for an Arab state. Many Arabs had fled those areas as well.) The United Nations Conciliation Commission for Palestine stated in 1951 that 711,000 Arabs had been displaced from Israel.

The circumstances of their displacement are the subject of heated debate. The PIDS routinely claim that all of the refugees were "expelled" and that there was a specific policy of ethnic cleansing by the Jewish leadership. But the charge of "ethnic cleansing" of Arabs by the Jews falls apart with a cursory look at the facts. Historians, such as Benny Morris, in his definitive book 1948, have documented that most Palestinian refugees fled without ever having seen an Israeli soldier. Elites of Palestinian society left immediately upon the United Nations' endorsement of partition in 1947, at the same time that fighters based in Arab villages began a campaign of attacks against the Jewish population. Many of the Arab villagers who intended to participate in such attacks sent their wives and children to live with family members in other villages in the British Mandate area or to other countries— Jordan, Syria and Lebanon. Others fled in fear of war, as civilians have done in war-torn areas for millennia. And in Haifa (as well as in parts of Jerusalem and elsewhere) the Arab population was instructed by the Arab

Higher Committee to flee. As *Time Magazine* reported on May 3, 1948: "The mass evacuation, prompted partly by fear, partly by order of Arab leaders, left the Arab quarter of Haifa a ghost city.... By withdrawing Arab workers their leaders hoped to paralyze Haifa." The Arabs of Haifa were threatened with being labeled as collaborators if they stayed. Other Arabs who fled were no doubt inspired by such threats.

The statistics that I will cite in the next paragraph are from Israeli-Palestinian ProCon (http://israelipalestinian.procon.org/) which is a neutral site that does not take positions on the issues and is run by advocates with neither a pro- or anti-Israel position. (Of course, you can hear the screams of "If you're not obviously against the racist-colonialist-Zionist-occupiers then we can't trust anything you say" from the PIDS. Just ignore them and focus on the facts; put the onus on the PIDS to disprove them.)

In 1946 "Palestine" (the British Mandate, comprising all the land between the Jordan River and the Mediterranean Sea) had 608,000 Jews and 1,237,000 Arabs (all statistics rounded to the nearest thousand). As a result of the war of attempted extermination launched by the Palestinian Arabs in 1947 and officially joined by the surrounding Arab countries in May 1948, there was a population exchange. The Arab refugee population mostly ended up in the West Bank and Gaza, usually imprisoned in UN-run refugee camps. The Jews who lived outside the area controlled by the IDF either fled as refugees to Israel or were killed. By 1949, Israel had 159,000 Arab citizens and 1,014,000 Jewish citizens.

In 1950, the nearest year for which population statistics are available, the West Bank and Gaza had 1,005,000 Arabs and no Jews-- it was a thoroughly ethnically cleansed area. Some towns like Hebron which had Jewish populations for centuries were actually emptied of their Jewish population long before the Partition Plan, as the result of pogroms. Some, like the Jewish Quarter of Jerusalem and the kibbutzim of the Etzion Bloc, were conquered by Arabs and the survivors forced to flee for their lives. At Kibbutz Kfar Etzion, over one hundred Jews were gunned down in cold blood by the Arabs in May 1948 after they had surrendered. While there were indeed documented incidents of expulsions of Arabs during Israel's War of Independence (one of which forms a central chapter of My Promised Land, the 2013 bestseller by Ari Shavit), the charge of wholesale ethnic cleansing is only true of the Arab side.

None of this eliminates the fact that Palestinians did indeed suffer displacement and dispossession as the result of the creation of Israel. Palestinians refer to this episode in their history as the "Nakba," Arabic for "catastrophe," and it is the core of their culture of victimhood. This can and should be acknowledged in any discussion—while pointing out that this catastrophe was caused by their own choice to fight the Jews rather than agree to live in peace alongside them, and by the decision by the surrounding Arab states (except for Jordan) to imprison the refugees in camps, denying them basic rights and the opportunity to assimilate into the society of their fellow Arabs with whom they shared common language, religion and culture.

The treatment of the Arab refugees is a matter that should bring shame to anyone who professes an allegiance to human rights. A United Nations administration, the United Nations Relief and Works Agency for Palestine Refugees in the Near East (UNRWA), was established for them. All other refugees from conflicts came under the auspices of the United Nations High Commissioner for Refugees (UNHCR) once it was established in 1950. UNHCR has the mandate to assist in the resettlement and assimilation of refugees when their return was not practical. UNRWA has no such mandate, because the Arab states (except for Jordan) refused to accept resettlement of the refugees, cynically preferring to keep their fellow Arabs in refugee camps as a demographic weapon against Israel. So rather than working to bring an end to their refugee status, UNRWA has perpetuated it not only by preserving that status, but also granting it to anyone descended from a male Palestinian refugee— forever. UNRWA has unilaterally decided that Palestinian refugee status even extends to 1.6 million descendants of refugees who are now Jordanian citizens, despite the fact that the UN's 1951 Convention Relating to the Status of Refugees notes that a refugee loses that status when acquiring the nationality of another country. Children in UNRWA schools are taught that their rightful place of residence is Israel itself, and that they will be "returning" there. There is now a fourth generation of children being raised from birth with this lie, constituting a major obstacle to peace. In Gaza, UNRWA not only employs Hamas members whose own Facebook pages include praise of Hitler and celebration of Hamas terrorism, its facilities have been used to store Hamas' weapons (which UNRWA helpfully returned to "the authorities"—Hamas!—once they were discovered) and as entrances for tunnels for Hamas fighters.

For those who spout "international law!" against every action Israel takes, it's noteworthy that nowhere in refugee law does the status of "refugee" (and access to funds, healthcare and education paid for disproportionately by the West, and only minimally by the Arabs themselves) become something carried in one's DNA and passed on to all of one's descendants for the rest of time. So while the issue of the actual refugees is a legitimate subject for discussions, over 99% of the current population referred to as "Palestinian refugees" does not even meet the minimal definition originally established by UNRWA: a person "whose normal place of residence was Palestine between June 1946 and May 1948, who lost both their homes and means of livelihood as a result of the 1948 Arab-Israeli conflict." This definition obviously includes economic migrants who had recently immigrated (legally or illegally) into Palestine from Egypt, Jordan and Syria, in addition to Arab families who did have a longer history in the area. Given that, it's really more appropriate in this discussion to set off the term with asterisks when referring to the Palestinian *refugee* population.

So while there are some tens of thousands of refugees still living, the bloated UNRWA registered *refugee* rolls list around five million. Given the 700% increase over the past 60 years, by mid-century the Palestinian *refugee* population will exceed that of Canada! Meanwhile, the UNHCR has only one fourth the staff of UNRWA, to assist the nearly 20 million actual refugees under its jurisdiction as of 2018.

One might think that the Arab countries, especially the oil sheikhdoms, would be funding this organization that essentially acts to prolong the conflict against Israel. But actually it's the taxpayers in the West who pay the bill for this counterproductive strategy. In 2012, the United States, European Union, United Kingdom, Sweden, Norway, Germany, the Netherlands and Japan together provided over 70% of the UNRWA budget. Saudi Arabia's contribution was half that of the Dutch. Qatar, which is spending over one hundred billion dollars on 2022 World Cup planning? Zero. It remains to be seen whether the Arab nations will make up for the US decision in August 2018 to de-fund UNRWA.

The reason given by the Arabs for their shabby treatment of their Arab brethren is that they demand the repatriation of the *refugees* to Israel itself, through a so-called "right of return." The utility of this demand was recognized by the Arab states quite early: Egyptian President Nasser stated in 1961 that "[i]f the Arabs return to Israel—Israel will cease to exist."

The "right of return" is the single biggest fraud promoted by PIDS. To understand why it's a fraud, look at the source they refer to: UN General Assembly Resolution 194, passed in December 1948. For those who didn't participate in Model UN programs in high school or college, General Assembly resolutions are not binding, and they don't constitute "international law."

Resolution 194 has a number of clauses, the relevant one being paragraph 11:

"Resolves that the refugees wishing to return to their homes and live at peace with their neighbors should be permitted to do so at the earliest practicable date, and that compensation should be paid for the property of those choosing not to return and for loss of or damage to property which, under principles of international law or in equity, should be made good by the Governments or authorities responsible.

Instructs the Conciliation Commission to facilitate the repatriation, resettlement and economic and social rehabilitation of the refugees and the payment of compensation, and to maintain close relations with the Director of the United Nations Relief for Palestine Refugees and, through him, with the appropriate organs and agencies of the United Nations."

You can loudly (and safely) offer the PIDS a large sum of money if they can find the word "right" anywhere in that paragraph. But wait, there's more: note that it refers to "refugees wishing to return home and live at peace with their neighbors." A large number of these *refugees* have been quite busy over the past few years building terror tunnels and launching rockets and arson kites from Gaza, which doesn't seem like they are people willing to live in peace with their neighbors.

The Conciliation Commission itself, in 1950, reviewed Resolution 194 and understood it as follows:

"What is the meaning of the term 'to their homes'? There is no doubt that in using this term the General Assembly meant the home of each refugee, i.e. his house or lodging and not his homeland. This is indicated by the fact that two amendments using the term 'the areas from which they have come' were rejected. Furthermore by implication it would appear that if the refugees not returning are to be compensated for their property, those returning would reoccupy their homes and be compensated only for losses and damages."[14]

Another salient point is that every single Arab member of the United Nations rejected this formulation and voted no on Resolution 194, because of other clauses which called for negotiations between the Arab states and Israel.

So now the PIDS solemnly proclaim that "international law" requires Israel to accept the influx of 5 million *refugees.*

---

[14] https://tinyurl.com/yc2tovcd

They even claim that Israel's admission to the United Nations stipulated this. Once again, reading the resolution itself is very revealing:

"Having received the report of the Security Council on the application of Israel for membership in the United Nations,

Noting that, in the judgment of the Security Council, Israel is a peace-loving State and is able and willing to carry out the obligations contained in the Charter,

Noting that the Security Council has recommended to the General Assembly that it admit Israel to membership in the United Nations,

Noting furthermore the declaration by the State of Israel that it "unreservedly accepts the obligations of the United Nations Charter and undertakes to honour them from the day when it becomes a Member of the United Nations",

Recalling its resolutions of 29 November 1947 and 11 December 1948 and taking note of the declarations and explanations made by the representatives of the Government of Israel before the Ad Hoc Political Committee in respect of the implementation of the said resolutions,

The General Assembly

Acting in discharge of its functions under Article 4 of the Charter and rule 125 of its rules of procedure,

1. Decides that Israel is a peace-loving State which accepts the obligations contained in the Charter and is able and willing to carry out those obligations;

2. Decides to admit Israel to membership in the United Nations."

No stipulations, no mention of any requirement upon Israel under the resolutions referred to (the partition plan and Resolution 194).

So to summarize, we have a demand for a "right of return" for *refugees* originating in a nonbinding resolution that was opposed by all the Arab states, which does not refer to any "rights" either for the actual refugees or for their descendants, and said "right" was not a requirement placed upon Israel when it was admitted to the UN. The "right of return" is the rainbow-colored unicorn of international law, but it has served as a very useful fiction for those activists and organizations whose underlying goal is opposing peace with Israel.

There is a recent example of an absolute "right of return" being rejected by an international law court. In 2010, the European Court of Human Rights denied a claim by Greek Cypriot refugees who fled the Turkish invasion of northern Cyprus in 1974. The Court noted that while they should be entitled to compensation for property that was left behind, the passage of time had made a "right of return" untenable. While that court has no jurisdiction outside of Europe, the precedent is certainly quite relevant—and quite unfavorable-- to the Palestinians' claim.

There's another side to the refugee issue that must not be forgotten: the Jewish refugees from Arab countries. PIDS will sometimes point out that Jews in Arab countries were far better off than their counterparts in Europe. That was certainly true-- in the 12th century. But the modern era was marked by riots in the 1930's in Egypt in support of the Nazis, the 1941 Farhud pogrom against the Jews of Iraq which killed nearly 300, and the 1945 pogrom in Tripoli, Libya killing 140.

Once the state of Israel was established, the Arab nations quickly began taking revenge upon their own Jewish citizens. Immediately upon the heels of the news of Israel's declaration of independence came the ominous headline in the New York Times of May 16, 1948: "Jews in Grave Danger in All Moslem Lands." The article described how Arab governments had already taken steps to limit the rights of Jews to travel and to conduct business, as well how anti-Semitic charges were being promoted in their government-controlled media.

As a result of persecutions, violence and expulsions, the Jews have now essentially disappeared from Arab countries. Egypt in 1948 had at least 75,000 Jews; today it has fewer than

100. Libya had over 35,000 in 1948, and Algeria 140,000; there are no Jews in either country today. Iraq had over 135,000 Jews; prior to the Second World War, a third of the city of Baghdad was Jewish. Today there are fewer than ten Iraqi Jews. Overall, from a population of over 850,000 in 1948, there are now fewer than 10,000 Jews in the entire Middle East and North Africa, outside of Israel.[15]

These Jewish communities were not waging war against their neighbors. They were hundreds of miles away, not participating in the conflict—Jews in the Arabized lands of the Middle East and North Africa weren't trying to drive their neighbors out of their homes or starve them into submission. They were victims of a deliberate policy of retaliation. (No, "Arabized lands" wasn't a typo. Think about it—until they were overrun by the Arab Islamic colonial-imperial project, these were lands that were populated by the indigenous people of the region: the Kurds, the Copts, the Yezidis, the Syriacs, the Amizigh—and the Jews. The Arabs turned them into "Arab lands" by the sword. Hat tip for that term to Canadian First Nations indigenous rights activist—and righteous Zionist— Ryan Bellerose.)

According to the World Organization of Jews from Arab Countries, the Jewish population of Arab countries has left behind title to land five times the size of the state of Israel and assets worth more than $300 billion dollars, confiscated by Arab governments.[16] Even if this figure is significantly inflated, those

---

[15] http://www.jewishvirtuallibrary.org/jsource/talking/jew_refugees.html

[16] http://www.jpost.com/JewishWorld/JewishNews/Article.aspx?id=82191

who suffered this consequence of deliberate ethnic cleansing are far more deserving of restitution and redress than the Palestinians who launched an attempted war of extermination against their neighbors.

These Jews fled to destinations around the globe. Most went to Israel, which, in stark contrast to the Arab treatment of Palestinian refugees, did integrate them into society, though that process was marred by discrimination. The majority of Israeli Jews now trace their heritage to the Islamic Middle East and North Africa. Others went to Europe and the United States. Very little international aid was provided to them, yet none remain stateless refugees today.

Anti-Israel groups will sometimes cynically suggest that these Jewish refugees (and, presumably, their descendants) should also be granted a "right of return" to the countries from which they fled persecution. They can do that knowing that very few Jews will want to leave Israel, the US or Europe to return to non-democratic countries in which the safety of non-Muslim minorities is at risk.

A comparison to other events of the mid-20th century is useful. One year before the creation of Israel, the British split their former colony of India into two parts: a state of India for the Hindus and a state of Pakistan for the Moslems. This partition was also not free of displacement and violence— hundreds of thousands were killed and 10-12 million people crossed borders (in both directions). Yet Hindu refugees were not locked into refugee camps by the Indians, nor were Moslem refugees by the Pakistanis (unlike Palestinians who were imprisoned by their fellow Arabs). And none have the status of refugees today.

Yet the Palestinian *refugees* remain in a state of limbo, supported mostly by the West (which pays the bulk of UNRWA's budget) while their fellow Arabs turn their backs on them. These *refugees* are paying the price for the decision made by their own leadership in 1947—to reject a state of their own in favor of an attempt to exterminate the Jewish population of Palestine, an attempt which even in failure cost the lives of one of every 100 Jews there. But the lesson of history has always been that there is no "do-over." There is no right to turn back the clock and say "we tried to destroy you and failed, but we must not suffer any consequences for this." There is no "right of return" for these *refugees*.

Human Rights: Unpack the Jargon of Jihad Hiding Behind the Language of Liberalism

Now if you thought the way the PIDS lie about Palestinian *refugees* is shameless, you'll be amazed at the way they surpass that with their slanders about Israel's record on human rights. They've taken the accusation of "ethnic cleansing" and further inflated it into the charge of "genocide" in the West Bank and Gaza. This statement is made not only in reference to Israel's military actions in Gaza but also with respect to Israel's settlement activities. Facts, once again, are your friends here.

The population of the West Bank in 1970 (prior to the re-establishment of any Jewish population in that area, outside of Jerusalem) was 677,000 Arabs--and no Jews. By 2003, the Arab population was 2,300,000 and the Jewish population was 219,000. Yes, that's right. The Arab population more than tripled over that time. In Gaza there were 368,000 Arabs in 1970; by 2003 there were 1,337,000. That's not a typo. Under the supposedly genocidal and tyrannical rule of Israeli occupation, the population of Gaza went up fourfold. In 2003, there were 7,500 Israeli Jews residing in Gaza. Now, of course, there are none.

During each of Israel's recent military actions in Gaza, the shrieks of "genocide" from the PIDS were all over social media and the public square. Yet you can calmly demonstrate that the evidence proves otherwise.

In each of those actions, half of the fatalities were determined—using Hamas' own casualty reports-- to be men of fighting age, 18 to 35. While women were 50% of the population, they were only 20% of the fatalities—and that included those being used as human shields as well as those deaths resulting from Hamas rockets falling short. If Israel was bombing indiscriminately, as the PIDS charge, then the casualties would reflect the makeup of the civilian population.

Typical military operations over the past 20 years (such as NATO bombing of Yugoslavia, and the US invasions of Iraq and Afghanistan) generate civilian casualties at three to four times the rate of combatants. The inescapable conclusion is that Israel took extraordinary measures to avoid civilian casualties, against an enemy that was hiding amongst civilians while simultaneously launching missiles against Israel's population centers. Colonel Richard Kemp, former commander of British forces in Afghanistan, testified to the UN Human Rights Council in 2009 that "during Operation Cast Lead, the Israeli Defense Forces did more to safeguard the rights of civilians in the combat zones than any other army in the history of warfare." Kemp reiterated this observation after Operations Pillar of Defense and Protective Edge.

Oh, but certainly in Jerusalem the Arabs are getting pushed out of their neighborhoods and ethnically cleansed, right? Sorry, once again those pesky facts get in the way. Let's look at the historical population of Jerusalem:

1946: 34,000 Muslims, 31,000 Christians, and 99,000 Jews (Yes, Jews were the majority in Jerusalem then, just as they had been since the late 19th century).

1967: 58,000 Muslims, 13,000 Christians, and 197,000 Jews

2000: 197,000 Muslims, 14,000 Christians and 440,000 Jews

Once again, the Muslim population has more than tripled since Israel re-unified the city!

Those crafty Zionists-- conducting ethnic cleansing but hiding it so well that the local Arab population doubles every 20 years. How do they pull it off? (No, I don't know either; the International Zionist Conspiracy hasn't given me that level of security clearance yet.)

Another point that the PIDS can't reconcile with their spurious claims of "genocide" is the treatment, in Israeli hospitals, of Palestinians from the West Bank and even from Gaza—at no charge. We're not talking about a few dozen people here. From the beginning of 2015 to the middle of 2016, over 360,000 permits were granted for Palestinians—including many from Gaza—to enter Israel for medical care. In May 2013, the Palestinian Minister of Health, Dr. Hanni Abadin, visited Hadassah Hospital in Jerusalem and visited Palestinian children hospitalized there. The hospital director noted that at any given time there are 60 Palestinian medical personnel in training at Hadassah. (Because, of course, that's all part of the nefarious

Zionist plot to eliminate the entire Palestinian people, through improved access to health care.)

The PIDS openly compare their efforts to the international movement against the actual apartheid regime in South Africa, and so have tried to slap this "scarlet letter" onto Israel itself. Now anyone who has been to Israel knows this is ludicrous—there are no buses, beaches, restaurants, hospitals or public facilities with signs that say "Jews only."

Arab and Jews at the Dead Sea (one of the many excellent posters in the "Apartheid?" series by the blogger Elder of Ziyon http://elderofziyon.blogspot.com/p/eoz-posters-for-apartheid-week.html)

The photograph below is an eloquent illustration of the completely false nature of this claim. Taken in the pediatric intensive care unit of Hadassah Hospital in September 2003, during Arafat's terror war, you can see an observant Jewish man in the foreground standing by his child's bedside, and in the background a woman in the Moslem hijab sitting by her child's bedside. That Arab child might have been an Israeli citizen from Nazareth or Jerusalem, or a Palestinian from Jenin or even from Gaza—and that child was getting the same care as the Jewish child.

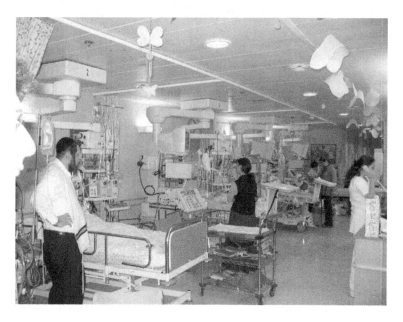

Photo by the author

Arab citizens of Israel have been represented in every Knesset since the founding of the state. There have been Arab justices on Israel's Supreme Court, and Arab diplomats have represented the State of Israel abroad. The presiding judge at the rape trial of former Israeli President Moshe Katzav was George Karra, an Arab from Jaffa.

source: Wikimedia Commons

Ismail Khaldi, former Deputy Consul General for the State of Israel in San Francisco. A Muslim Arab. (He clearly didn't get the memo about Israel being "apartheid.")

Does Israel's Arab population share equally in the economy? No. Neither do the ultra-Orthodox Jews. Both communities are marked by problems endemic to poorer families in every community in the world: larger families, less educational achievement, and yes, discrimination. There is indeed discrimination in the work force in Israel against ultra-Orthodox Jews.

News flash: racism against Arabs does exist in Israel-- just as racism against African-Americans and Hispanic-Americans exists in the United States, just as racism against Arabs exists in France, just as racism against Turks exists in Germany, just as racism against Jews exists, well, almost everywhere. And while media outlets feast on completely inexcusable acts of violence and intimidation aimed at Israel's Arab citizens, there is a small country in which over 100 mosques were vandalized (many by arson) between 2005 and 2010. Yet one doesn't see the Netherlands routinely charged with being a "racist state."[17] But the comparison to apartheid-era South Africa-- in which the educational and employment opportunities for the black majority were limited by law, in which public facilities were segregated by law, and in which the majority was not given the right to vote for those who governed it—is not only ludicrous, it's a malignant slander. While I doubt that 60% of black South Africans under apartheid had a positive view of their country, in a September 2017 poll 60% of Arab citizens expressed a positive view of Israel.[18] And a majority of them described themselves as "Israeli" rather than "Palestinian."

The charge of "apartheid" is often coupled with the charge that Israel is a "settler-colonial" state, in the model of European colonies that were established across much of Africa and Asia in the 19th century—run for the economic benefit of the home office in London, Paris or Berlin and without rights of self- governance for the indigenous peoples. This overlooks the unique situation of the Jewish people who were returning to their own historic homeland, and leaving the lands of Europe behind due to persecution and violence, rather than carrying the flags of those nations. Although political Zionism did indeed result in a mostly European population of Jews during the pre-

---

[17] www.ynetnews.com/articles/0,7340,L-4586532,00.html

[18] https://www.jpost.com/Israel-News/Survey-60-percent-of-Arab-Israelis-have-positive-view-of-state-506150

state years, Israel has subsequently become a multiethnic country in which people whose recent heritage is from the Middle East and Africa—including Arabs-- are the majority.

The attempt to label Israel as racist revives the infamous "Zionism is racism" resolution that passed the United Nations General Assembly in 1975, marking the point at which that body finally lost the last shreds of moral authority it had with regard to the Middle East; even the repeal of that obscene statement in 1991 could not restore it. Proponents of this distorted view of Zionism claim that it sought—and still seeks-- an exclusively Jewish state, or a state in which non-Jews would be relegated to second-class citizenship. Don't hesitate to remind your audience of the truth: Zionism is the national movement of the Jewish people to establish its own nation in a part of its historic homeland.

What about the charge that the Jews aren't a people, "just" a religion, and therefore not deserving of our own state? Not only does this ignore the existence of 56 Islamic states but more importantly, it ignores the unique nature of the Jewish people. Our history is more than religious belief—those beliefs and practices are inseparable from our historic ties to the specific land from which they arose. Jews the world over face Jerusalem to pray, and in Jerusalem they face the Temple Mount. In every set of daily prayers, Jews for centuries have prayed for a return to the land of Israel. And at our holiest moments of the year—the end of Yom Kippur as the shofar is blown, and the end of the Passover Seder which retells the founding of the Jewish nation, we sing "L'shana haba'a b'Yerushalayim"—"next year in Jerusalem."

Is this claim to the land based solely on the Bible? No, although for some Jewish and Christian supporters of Israel, that claim is sufficient. Rather, it's based on history. Our ancestors literally carved their legacy into the land. Buildings, coins and other artifacts from the First Temple era, over 600 years prior to the Roman era, attest to the ancient Jewish history of the land. Histories of the time describe the Jewish kingdoms. The Arch of Titus in Rome commemorates the Roman destruction of the Second Temple.

All this vitiates the complaint that the Palestinians were made to pay the price for Europe's genocide against its Jewish population. Indigenous status and history are justification for the establishment of the modern Jewish state; the Holocaust demonstrated (with extreme horror) the consequences of the lack of one. The connected spring commemorations in Israel one week apart—Yom Hashoah (Holocaust Memorial Day) and Yom Hazikaron (Memorial Day for fallen soldiers and victims of terror), are twin reminders of the costs of not having a state, and the price of having one.

PIDS will also charge that Ashkenazic Jews (from Europe) are not historically Jewish, being descended from the Russian Khazars, a theory that was invented by the novelist and journalist Arthur Koestler in his 1976 book <u>The Thirteenth Tribe</u>. They state that Ashkenazim are therefore not part of the Jewish people and have no claim to the Jewish homeland. Aside from the outrageousness of someone else trying to define the Jewish people to fit their own narrow political aims, science also proves them wrong. The New York Times published an article in June 2010, "Studies Show Jews' Genetic Similarity" which noted: "A major surprise from both surveys is the genetic closeness of the two Jewish communities of Europe, the Ashkenazim and the Sephardim. Ashkenazic and Sephardic Jews have roughly 30 percent European ancestry, with most of the rest from the Middle East, the two surveys find."[19]

So as an Ashkenazic Jew, I am far more closely related to a Sephardic Jew than I am to my own grandparents' Polish and Ukrainian non-Jewish neighbors. Yet PIDS deny the legitimacy of 2000 years of history of the Jewish people in Europe, who maintained –and also suffered and died for—their Jewish faith, while insisting that any descendant of an Arab who lived for two years in British Palestine be forever considered a Palestinian.

As Yossi Klein Halevi notes in his 2018 book <u>Letters To My Palestinian Neighbor,</u> "So long as Palestinian leaders insist on defining the Jews as a religion rather than allowing us to define ourselves as we have since ancient times—as a people with a particular faith—then Israel will continue to be seen as illegitimate, its existence an open question." So if I am asked to recognize rights of a Palestinian people—who did not appear on the world stage as such until the past century, having left no mark on the historical record prior to that—then I insist on the recognition of the same rights for the Jewish people, a society that has existed for over 3000 years with a unique language, unique history, and ties to a single homeland.

Are there some ways in which Jews and non-Jews are not treated equally under the law in Israel? Yes. One of the most important is the Law of Return, which allows anyone with a Jewish grandparent to immigrate to Israel and have an automatic right to citizenship. This is one of the practical expressions of Israel being the nation-state of the Jewish people.

---

[19] http://www.nytimes.com/2010/06/10/science/10jews.html?_r=0

It doesn't discriminate against Arab citizens of Israel, but only affects those who might become citizens. From reading anti-Israel screeds, one would never know that immigration preferences for repatriation of a diaspora population are quite common in the world today. The legal term for this right is *lex sanguinis*. Countries that provide such preferences include Armenia (another country with a widespread diaspora), China, Finland, Germany, Greece, Hungary, India, Ireland, Italy, Japan, Poland, Romania, Russia and Spain. This covers a pretty fair-sized chunk of the world's population. Given that none of these countries (except Armenia) can document any history of genocidal persecution in its diaspora similar to what the Jewish people have experienced, why is only Israel singled out as if its immigration law is unique?

Israel's new nation-state law passed in 2018 raised the ire of the PIDS to stratospheric levels. To be fair, this bill is controversial even within the pro-Israel community, due to several provisions: one dealing with relations between Israel and the Jewish diaspora that could be a barrier to advancing the rights of non-Orthodox Jews in Israel, and the downgrading the status of the Arabic language from "official" to "special status", creating concern about the effect on Jewish-Arab relations within Israel. But the outrage from the PIDS stems from Israel enacting, with the force of law, what has been the truth from its first day of existence—its status as the nation-state of the Jewish people. The very first section of the bill reads:

"The State of Israel
a) Israel is the historical homeland of the Jewish people in which the state of Israel was established.
b) The state of Israel is the nation-state of the Jewish people, in which it actualizes its natural, religious, and historical right for self-determination.

c) The actualization of the right of national self-determination in the state of Israel is unique to the Jewish people."

This doesn't change anything on the ground in Israel. Nobody lost voting rights, civil rights, or any of the many other rights that Israel provides to all of its citizens.

The bill also enshrines into law Israel's flag, the menorah as the national symbol and Hatikvah as the national anthem. PIDS charge that these are discriminatory and must be changed so as not to show any preference to Jews and Judaism.

Yet the flag of the Ottoman Empire has been an inspiration for the flag designs of many other Muslim nations. The Ottoman crescent became associated with Islam and now appears on the flags of Algeria, Azerbaijan, Comoros, Malaysia, Mauritania, Pakistan, Tunisia, Turkey and the Turkish Republic of Northern Cyprus.

The Saudi Arabian flag is much more direct:

The Arabic text reads: "There is no god but God and Muhammad is the messenger of God". (Nope, nothing religious there at all.)

These countries all feature a different religious symbol, the Christian cross, on their flags:

Denmark, Finland, Iceland, Norway, Sweden, Switzerland, Greece and Tonga.

Yet only Israel is pilloried for using the symbol of the Jewish people on its flag.

As for national anthems, here are selections from some national anthems that somehow are not vilified as "racist" or for religious content–

Saudi Arabia:

"Hasten to glory and supremacy! Glorify the Creator of the heavens And raise the green, fluttering flag, Carrying the emblem of Light! God is greatest! O my country, My country, may you always live, The glory of all Muslims! Long live the King, For the flag and the country!"

Romania:

"Priests, lead with your crucifixes, for our army is Christian,

The motto is Liberty and its goal is holy"

Poland:

"Poland has not yet died,

So long as we still live.

What the foreign power has seized from us,

We shall recapture with a sabre."

Thailand (I'm not criticizing Thailand here, but I wonder how the Chinese and Malay minorities in Thailand feel about this anthem):

"Thailand unites its people with flesh and blood. The land of Thailand belongs to the Thais....."

The mention of the Jewish soul's hope to become a nation in its own land isn't so different, is it?

In its government, Israel does not have religious restrictions similar to those in force in many other nations. Not only is Judaism not enshrined as the state religion, but Israel is not one of the thirty countries that as of 2014 required their heads of state to belong to a specific religion.[20] (Though seventeen Muslim nations were on that list!)

As for land itself, the charge is frequently leveled against Israel that the laws covering land ownership discriminate against Arabs. To refute this claim requires an understanding of the historical situation.

When Israel was founded, most of the land in the state had actually been owned by the government—first by the

---

[20] http://www.pewresearch.org/fact-tank/2014/07/22/in-30-countries-heads-of-state-must-belong-to-a-certain-religion/

Ottomans, then by the British, then by the State of Israel. One of the specious claims made by PIDS is that since the Jews only owned 7% of the land at the time of the UN partition resolution, the rest was "Arab land." This claim is illustrated in maps that have spread like a malignant fungus throughout the Internet and even onto ads placed on public transit in various cities in North America:

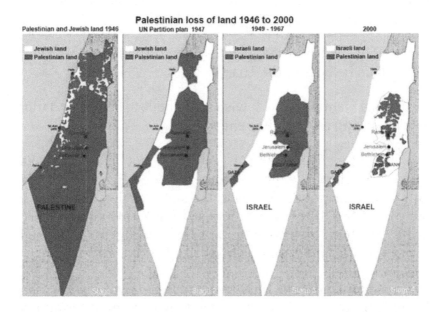

Actually, over 70% of the land under the Mandate was government owned. So most of that area marked as "Palestinian" would properly be colored with the red, blue and white of the Union Jack—and after 1948 with the blue and white of the State of Israel. This postcard from StandWithUs debunks these lies:

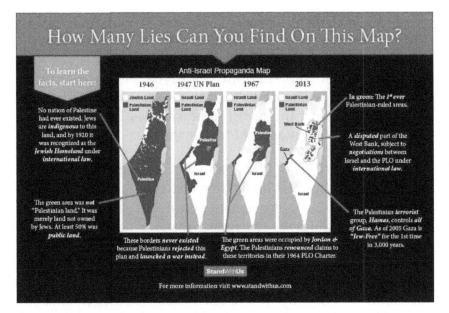

You can download this at:
http://www.standwithus.com/postcards/?wc=6.

In Israel today, most of the land remains under state ownership and is leased to private owners—Arabs as well as Jews. This includes land that was purchased by the Jewish National Fund during the pre-state era. This was funded by private donations from Jews throughout the world. Those lands were purchased in trust by—and for—the Jewish people. From 1960 until 2000, JNF lands were administered by the state and, because of the conditions of their purchase, leases were indeed reserved for Jewish communities only. This was changed in 2000 after Israel's Supreme Court ruled that this was inconsistent with the values of a Jewish and democratic state and now those, like other state lands, are legally leased by Israeli Arabs as well as Jews.

When challenged with these facts about Israeli history, land and society, some of the PIDS will try to walk back the "Apartheid" label and (almost inaudibly) admit that Israeli Arab citizens are not subjected to that type of discrimination. However, they will charge that the situation in Judea and Samaria —in which the Jewish minority has control over the Arab majority—is tantamount to apartheid.

Once again, facts are a great neutralizer of poisonous lies. While Arabs in the West Bank are not citizens of Israel, they are indeed a population living in an area which is partially occupied by Israel. They do have the right to vote—in elections of the Palestinian Authority (whenever those might occur again...). And 95% of the Palestinian population of the West Bank lives under the rule of the PA. But the unequal situation in this area is not based on ethnicity. It's based instead on citizenship. For example, there are no "Jewish only roads" (a common charge of the PIDS) but there are "Israeli only roads" that were built in the past decade because of Palestinian terrorism.

Is this current situation sustainable in the long-term? Highly unlikely. But PIDS who throw around the "A" word aren't interested in ending Israel's occupation by a peace agreement that would create a Palestinian state living in peace with the Jewish one. They have a far different solution in mind; that's the next chapter.

Key points:

Israel is not required by international law to turn over ALL of Judea and Samaria to the Palestinians.

Settlements are one obstacle to peace among many, and not the major one.

The major obstacle to peace is the Palestinian refusal to accept the existence of a Jewish state at all; their manipulation of the Palestinian refugee issue from 1948 to today is part of that.

There was a larger population of Jewish refugees that were deliberately persecuted and expelled by Arab nations as a reprisal for the creation of Israel.

The situation of Arabs in Israel is in no way comparable to that of blacks in apartheid-era South Africa.

Chapter 7: One State to Rule Them All

For every complex problem there is an answer that is clear, simple, and wrong.– HL Mencken

In Tolkien's "Lord of the Rings" saga, the Dark Lord Sauron forged the "One Ring to rule them all." The PIDS have come up with an equally sinister variation on this theme, with a specific solution for the seemingly intractable problem of the Middle East. At one point, forty years ago, they called for an independent Palestinian state in the West Bank and Gaza, knowing full well that such a state would be a base from which the PLO would launch more terror attacks against Israel. Once the Palestinians did achieve a measure of self-rule (and then predictably followed up that autonomy with far more terror attacks against Israeli civilians), they moved the goalposts— right into the waters of the Mediterranean. Instead of a

Palestinian state alongside Israel, their demand is now for "one democratic state from the river to the sea."

Sometimes PIDS will attempt to hide this goal by expressing support for a Palestinian state in Gaza and the West Bank "as a start" or "for now" (a response that has the same level of integrity as an e-mail from a Nigerian prince asking you for your bank account information so you can help him transfer his multimillion-dollar fortune out of Africa).

Superficially, "one democratic state" sounds like a much more user-friendly position (at least in America) than the cry, "Filastin arduna wa al-yahud kilabuna!" ("Palestine is our land and the Jews are our dogs!") This hateful chant, which the Grand Mufti's rioters offered up during the 1920 Nebi Musa pogrom in Jerusalem, has been heard in the United States at anti-Israel rallies within the past twenty years. But their ultimate objective is the same as the one-state plan. In many ways PIDS treat Israel like the "Fight Club" (in the movie of the same name): The first rule of Israel is there is no Israel.

Population figures and a little simple math clarify their objective:

At its 70th birthday in 2018, Israel had just over 8.8 million people of whom 75% (6.6 million) were Jews, 21% (1.8 million) Arab, and the rest a variety of other ethnicities.

Population figures in the West Bank and Gaza Strip are less reliable as there has not been a census taken there. It is estimated by Sergio DellaPergola, a demographer from Jerusalem's Hebrew University, that these areas contain about 4.7 million Arabs (about half of whom are considered

Palestinian *refugees* by UNRWA).[21] About 1.8 million of these are in Gaza, and the rest live in the West Bank and the eastern part of Jerusalem across the Green Line.

As of 2015, Palestinian *refugees* living outside of Israel, the West Bank and Gaza, who under this "one-state" plan would be given the "right to return," number about three million people.

Put them all together in one dystopian entity and you have a state with 9.5 million Arabs and 6.6 million Jews. The sad truth is that the world has had extensive experience with states where rival ethnic groups continue to live together in intermittently erupting fury (consider Iraq, Lebanon, Bahrain, Nigeria, and Georgia for starters) or fall apart in bloody civil war (not just Syria, but also the former Yugoslavia, and its progeny Bosnia and Serbia), or have explosions of savage genocide (hello, Rwanda). Other such countries have fallen apart relatively peacefully into new states based more on national, ethnic or religious grounds (think Czechoslovakia or most of the former Soviet Union). But whether peacefully or violently, the trend is for individual national or ethnic groups to seek to determine their own destiny in their own nation-states.

The history of the Jewish people, while in exile from their homeland, validates their concerns about living as a stateless minority. The history of the Jews in Europe has been marked by expulsions (Britain in 1190 and Spain in 1492), pogroms (from the period of the Crusades into the 20th century in Russia), and

---

[21] https://www.timesofisrael.com/expert-confirms-jews-and-arabs-nearing-population-parity

second class citizenship (until the Napoleonic Era). This culminated in the gas chambers of Auschwitz, while the rest of the world closed their doors to Jewish refugees and there was no Jewish state to offer them refuge. While the history of the Jews in Arabized lands has had its better moments, those moments took place centuries ago—and the modern experience of Jews in Arab lands hounded en masse into emigration shows that Jews cannot consider themselves safe and secure as a minority in the Middle East. Even today, the track record of Muslim Arab states when it comes to tolerating Christians, or even Muslims of different sects (who are currently conducting a medieval war with high tech weapons in Yemen, the flashpoint of the greater Sunni-Shiite rivalry between Saudi Arabia and Iran, respectively), does not provide any reassurance for the fate of Jews in a potential "one state" scenario.

And despite halting movements toward democracy that may be taking place in the Arab world, the type of "democracy" seen all too frequently throughout the region is "one man, one vote, once," in which the party winning the occasional election then takes power and refuses to hold another one. (Let's also not forget that women don't get to vote in most of the Arab regimes.) There's no reason to think the Arab majority of the bastard state "Isratine" (a term coined by the late Libyan dictator and bad hair archetype Muammar Ghaddafi) would be any more tolerant of gays, journalists, or political dissidents than the "moderate" (cough, cough) government of the Palestinian Authority (much less Hamas).

The goal of the "one democratic state" proposal is actually very straightforward—to turn the entire region of historic Palestine (between the Jordan River and the Mediterranean Sea) into the twenty-second Arab state, and to strip the Jewish people of their own national rights in their homeland. But doesn't it sound much less malignant when couched in the language of "democracy?"

There's also another dance known as "two-state doublespeak." When supporters of Israel talk about two states, we refer to one state for the Jewish people and one state for the Palestinian Arabs; in short, two states for two peoples. This is exactly what the UN endorsed in the 1947 partition plan – independent Jewish and Arab states. Some PIDS, as well as Palestinian Authority leaders and spokespeople, have also used the term "two state solution." But if you listen carefully, they're not talking about a Jewish state and an Arab state. Throughout the negotiations between Israel and the Palestinian Authority in 2013-14, and in his public statements since, Mahmoud Abbas was resolute in his refusal both to accept Israel as the state of the Jewish people and to renounce the claim of return for the Palestinian *refugees.* He gave every impression that his version of a two-state solution has one state in the West Bank and Gaza (which will be a Palestinian Arab state in which no Jews may live), while the other state will be within the borders of pre-1967 Israel but will no longer be a Jewish state—because it will be forced to accept the five million Palestinian *refugees* from outside its borders and thus become a smaller and more crowded "binational state."

Does anyone seriously think Jews and Arabs in that binational state will be sitting on the hilltops singing "Kumbaya" together while watching the sun set into the Mediterranean Sea? After all, many of these returning *refugees* are the same people who have been launching tens of thousands of rockets at Israeli civilians throughout the past decade. Even many of the people proposing this "solution" don't believe it will lead to peace. But they don't really care, because peace isn't their objective. As Ali Abunimah, founder of the "Electronic Intifada" website who promoted the one state scenario in his book <u>One Country</u>, admitted the potential outcome of his proposal: "We couldn't rule out some disastrous situation like Zimbabwe."[22]

It's also very telling that while many proponents of the one-state plan oppose the very existence of a Jewish state because they believe that "a state shouldn't be based on a religion," none of them are agitating for the elimination of any of the dozens of nations which proudly declare themselves to be based on the Islamic faith.

Of course, the reality is that even creating this fantasy state without massive bloodshed faces towering obstacles. The foremost among them is that more than 85% of Jewish Israelis are opposed to losing their national sovereignty.[23] Since Jews comprise 75% of the population of Israel, that's a solid majority of Israeli citizens who would reject subsuming their national identity into this chimera. But for the "peace and justice activists" that promote the one-state fantasy, the democratic preferences of Israeli citizens don't matter. Palestinian Arabs themselves also reject it: in a March 2018 poll, 69% of Palestinians opposed the idea of "one state in which Palestinians and Jews will be citizens of the same state and enjoy equal rights." [24] You might well ask whose interests these activists

---

[22] http://www.ngo-monitor.org/article/electronic_intifada_and_ali_abunimah_factsheet

[23] http://israelipalestinian.procon.org/view.answers.php?questionID=000565

[24] http://www.pcpsr.org/en/node/725

actually represent, and how they would propose to impose this solution on two populations who both reject it.

During his first presidential campaign in 1932, Franklin Roosevelt stated: "Judge me by the enemies I have made." Not surprisingly, the lineup of those who support the fraudulent "one-state solution" is a cast of Sith Lords straight out of Star Wars. They include Iran's former president and Holocaust-denier Mahmoud Ahmedinejad (as well as all other Iranian leaders since the 1979 Islamist revolution), Hamas strongmen Yahya Sinwar, Khaled Meshal and Ismail Haniyeh, as well as the late (and unlamented, except by the aforementioned Hamas) Osama bin Laden. Given that list, perhaps this plan should more accurately be named the "one-state final solution."

On the positive (Jedi knights) side, those who endorse the concept of two states for two peoples include the United States under both George W. Bush and Barack Obama, all of the European Union's national leaders, as well as every Israeli Prime Minister since Ehud Barak in 2000. It's definitely a friendlier group to invite to your dinner party.

Key points:

The "one-state solution" would end Jewish rights of national self-determination.

The overwhelming majority of Israelis oppose the one-state solution, which means that it ignores the rights of the people of Israel to democratically determine their own future.

History shows us that forcing separate ethnic groups with a long record of conflict to live under one government is a recipe for constant discord at best and disaster at worst.

A one-state solution would create another Muslim Arab majority state which would not guarantee the rights or even the safety of its non-Muslim inhabitants.

Chapter 8: UNfair, UNjust and UNrepentant [the UN's fatal bias against Israel]

Most of the voting in the U.N. is for non-binding resolutions that hold no weight. It's like internet polls with more Jew-hating.- - Frank J Fleming[25]

When it comes to Israel, the UN has the tenacity of a small terrier working its favorite chew toy. The reason for this has been well established: the automatic majority of states that because of oil, Islam, or "stick it to The Man" anti-Americanism will vote yes on almost any anti-Israel resolution. While the PIDS will certainly refer to UN resolutions as if they constituted the findings of an august body of impartial legislators, the UN membership is mostly comprised of despotic governments that

---

[25] http://www.imao.us/docs/about_imao.html

don't even answer to their own people, much less to any standard of human rights.

The UN, with regard to Israel, is the institutional embodiment of double standards. More accurately, as Israel's former UN Ambassador Ron Prosor put it, the UN actually has a triple set of standards: one for dictatorships, one for democracies and one for Israel. The UN's record on human rights includes these highlights (you couldn't make this stuff up if you tried):

● Electing Muammar Ghaddafi's Libya to a seat on the Security Council in 2008 and the Human Rights Council in 2009

● Praising Sri Lanka's human rights record in the aftermath of a bloody civil war against Tamil rebels that killed 40,000 and turned tens of thousands more into homeless refugees.

● Electing Iran to the UN Commission on the Status of Women in 2010 and again in 2014. Then, presumably for balance, electing Saudi Arabia in 2017.

● Having Iran, while under Security Council sanctions for its nuclear weapons program, chair the Disarmament Commission in June 2013 and electing it to a leadership position in the First Committee (which deals with disarmament) in September 2013.

● Allowing Sudan, whose president was under indictment by the International Criminal Court, to chair meetings of the Economic and Social Council in July 2013. ECOSOC is the body that oversees the UN human rights commissions.

• Having a permanent agenda item on the Human Rights Council entitled "the Human Rights Situation in Palestine and Other Occupied Arab Territories."—the only such country-specific item.

• Accrediting the Perdana Global Peace Foundation, founded by Malaysia's former Prime Minister Matathir Mohammed, who stated in 2003 "The Jews rule the world by proxy" and followed that up in 2012 by stating "I am glad to be labeled an anti-Semite." Which UN body accredited Perdana? The UN Committee on the Exercise of the Inalienable Rights of the Palestinian People.

• In May 2014, adopting one country-specific resolution in the UN World Health Assembly, criticizing Israel for actions that allegedly harmed the health of Palestinians. Syria, whose leader was busy dropping shrapnel-filled "barrel bombs" and using chlorine gas on his own countrymen, accused Israel of "inhumane practices that target the health of Syrian citizens."

• In May 2018, having Syria, while busily engaged in chemical weapons attacks on its own people, chair the UN Conference on Disarmament, the very body which produced the 1993 treaty banning chemical weapons.

• And, of course, passing a resolution declaring that Zionism is a form of racism and then taking 16 years to remove that stain from the record.

The United Nations Human Rights Council features dictatorial regimes such as Cuba and North Korea complimenting other autocracies such as Syria on their human rights records, and two standing agenda items for assessing human rights—one for Israel and one for the other 192 member states. This means that elected members such as the slave-labor state of Qatar and the brutally oppressive dictatorship of Venezuela sit in judgment of Israel. In 2017, the UNHCR even launched an investigation into the "exclusion of women" in Israeli society. (I don't know if they took comments from women in many parts of the Muslim world who are denied an education and forced to veil their faces.)

Even UN Secretary-General Kofi Annan admitted in 2006 "On one side, supporters of Israel feel that it is harshly judged by standards that are not applied to its enemies. And too often this is true, particularly in some UN bodies." In August 2013, Secretary-General Ban Ki-Moon acknowledged that Israel has "suffered from bias—and sometimes even discrimination" within the organization. In 2013, a UN interpreter (thinking she was off-mic and speaking only to colleagues) accidentally broadcast the following to the entire General Assembly and a worldwide webcast audience: "I think when you have... like a total of ten resolutions on Israel and Palestine, there's gotta be something, c'est un peu trop, non? [It's a bit much, no?] I mean I know... There's other really bad shit happening, but no one says anything about the other stuff." [26] Abba Eban, perhaps Israel's most famous diplomat in the first decades of its existence, accurately summarized it: "If Algeria introduced a resolution declaring that the earth was flat and that Israel had flattened it, it would pass by a vote of 164 to 13 with 26 abstentions."

Israel's dysfunctional relationship with the UN dates almost from the very beginning of the state. In 1955, David Ben-Gurion's famously disdainful "Oom-Shmoom" ("Oom" being the

---

[26] https://www.unwatch.org/u-n-interpreter-falls-victim-dreaded-hot-mic/

Hebrew acronym for the UN) reflected resentment that the UN had failed to condemn terror attacks against Israel launched from Gaza, yet the international body found its collective voice in time to condemn Israel for reprisal raids against the perpetrators of these atrocities (sound familiar?). And when Jordan immediately violated the terms of the 1949 Armistice Agreement which stated that there would be free access to the Western Wall and other holy sites, the UN's response was a deafening silence.

The historian Ephraim Karsh noted that

"[t]he UN rarely calls for emergency special sessions and did not see any reason to hold such a meeting to discuss genocide in Rwanda, ethnic cleansing in Yugoslavia, genocide in Darfur or the horrific massacres in East Timor. But in 2003 alone, it felt the need to call an unprecedented three emergency sessions—two to condemn Israel's security barrier and one to criticize Israel for considering (considering, not even carrying out!!) the expulsion of Arafat."[27]

There are three separate special entities within the UN to promote the Palestinian cause. The Special Committee to Investigate Israeli Practices Affecting the Human Rights of the Palestinian People and Other Arabs of the Occupied Territories, the Committee on the Exercise of the Inalienable Rights of the Palestinian People, and the Division for Palestinian Rights (DPR) within the Secretariat. Every November 29 (the anniversary of the adoption of the 1947 partition plan by the General Assembly) the DPR organizes the International Day of Solidarity

---

[27] http://www.meforum.org/3299/war-against-jews

with the Palestinian People. The message delivered by the DPR, without any subtlety, is that only the Palestinians are victims-- and only the Zionists are the aggressors, responsible for the Palestinian refugee population.

The UN bureaucracy is itself riddled with sketchy characters, not limited to those staffing the entities charged with promoting the Palestinian cause:

Richard Falk, the former "UN Special Rapporteur on the situation of human rights in the Palestinian territories occupied since 1967," has promoted the conspiracy theory that the attacks of September 11, 2001 were perpetrated by the United States government. Falk was so active in promoting Hamas that even the Palestinian Authority called upon him to quit his post.

Falk's successor, Michael Lynk, brought his own uniquely skewed outlook on "human rights" to his position. Among those he praised as "human rights defenders" were Mohammed el-Halabi, arrested by Israel for diverting $50 million from the World Vision charity to Hamas, and Manal Tamimi (part of the family that has produced Ahlam Tamimi, who masterminded the 2001 Jerusalem Sbarro pizzeria bombing that killed 15 people, half of them children) who has tweeted sentiments such as "we will keep resisting until the last Zionist either got killed or leave Palestine."[28]

Alfred de Zayas, another top staffer at the Human Rights Council, has his writings featured on Holocaust denial websites and claims that the Germans were the victims, and the Allies the

---

[28] https://www.ngo-monitor.org/reports/united-nations-human-rights-defenders-2017/

perpetrators, of genocide. On an official UN trip to Venezuela in 2017, he posted (and later deleted) regime propaganda photos denying mass hunger—while children were dying of starvation there.

Jean Ziegler, the former UN Special Rapporteur on the Right to Food, was a leader of a consortium of organizations that in 1989 created the Muammar Ghaddafi Prize for Human Rights. He was given this award himself in 2002; other "winners" include French Holocaust denier Roger Garaudy. While ignoring food emergencies around the world, Ziegler has always been ready to publicly advocate against the United States and Israel. In 2013, he was rewarded by being nominated (by Switzerland) to be an adviser to the UN Human Rights Council in Geneva.

Jean-Paul Laborde, appointed in 2013 to head the UN's Counter-Terrorism Directorate, said in 2010 that Hamas was not a terrorist organization.

And carrying the UN's reputation on the cultural side is UN Goodwill Ambassador Majida El Roumi, a singer from Lebanon. In 2016 she told an audience at Beirut Arab University about reading the Protocols of the Elders of Zion as a child, and how it informed her worldview that "global Zionism has a plan to fragment the Arab world."[29]

Of course, the UN is also responsible for the operations of the United Nations Relief and Works Agency for Palestine Refugees in the Near East (UNRWA), whose mandate to continue the *refugee* status of Palestinians is one of the major

---

[29] https://www.memri.org/tv/lebanese-singer-majida-el-roumi-global-zionism-implementing-protocols-of-elders-of-zion-plot

obstacles to peace. UNRWA further throws gasoline on the fire by operating schools in which the most extreme anti-Israel propaganda is taught, especially in Gaza where many UNRWA employees are also members of Hamas. During Operation Protective Edge (as well as the previous Gaza operations), the IDF documented the launch of rockets from UNRWA schools, which were also being used for storage of missiles by Hamas. UNRWA was proud that its staff contacted the local authorities to dispose of them; of course, the "local authorities" who took custody of the missiles were Hamas. At least one booby-trapped tunnel built by Hamas also used an UNRWA clinic as an access point.

Yet, despite stiff competition, the award for "Most Outrageous Statement" contest that the UN appeared to be holding during Operation Protective Edge goes to Navi Pillay, who was at the time the chair of the UN Human Rights Council. Pillay filled her tenure with a lengthy history of biased criticisms of Israel. Just one day after the start of Operation Cast Lead in 2008, she had already declared Israel guilty of war crimes! Pillay also defended Richard Falk against those who criticized his use of anti-Semitic memes, and sought to investigate the United States for not having taken Osama bin Laden alive (thus joining Hamas in condemning his elimination). She was also responsible for the travesty that was the Goldstone Report, prepared by a committee that had declared Israel guilty of war crimes in Operation Cast Lead before even starting its "investigation." But saving her best for last, in 2014 she criticized the United States for not having provided the protection of Israel's anti-missile system Iron Dome to Hamas. Rather than condemn Hamas for launching rockets from populated areas (and killing an unknown number of civilians when their rockets fell short of Israel, as hundreds of them did), she wanted to provide better protection for the terror group to continue firing from those areas.

Chapter 1, Article 2 of the UN Charter states that it is "based on the principle of sovereign equality of its members" and that "all members shall refrain in their international relations from the threat or use of force against the territorial integrity or political independence of any state." Yet as we have seen here, some of its own agencies delegitimize the very existence of one of its own members.

So, given the automatic majority of members for whom voting against Israel is as natural a function as breathing, and for whom "human rights" are important only as a weapon against Israel (but not for their own citizens), does the preponderance of anti-Israel resolutions at the UN make a statement about Israel-- or is it more of a judgment upon the UN itself?

Key point: the UN, because of its predominance of Muslim and anti-Western countries that don't respect the human rights of their own citizens, is terminally biased against Israel. Its moral standing to speak out on human rights is equivalent to that of the Ku Klux Klan to condemn others for racism.

Chapter 9: Is It Anti-Semitism?

"The fun thing about being Jewish, whether in individual or state form, is that people think it's OK to talk about whether you should exist." Yair Rosenberg (@Yair_Rosenberg), Twitter, 9/7/17

The PIDS are quick to fall back on a favorite trope when their lies are challenged: "Anytime we criticize Israel, you claim that it is anti-Semitic." This attempt to deflect any substantive criticism of their misleading and misinformed statements is also an attempt by the PIDS to turn themselves into victims being unfairly accused of a venal hatred. Sometimes they'll also try to deflect the argument into the linguistically irrelevant "But Arabs are Semites too, and I'm pro-Palestinian, so I can't be anti-Semitic!" (The term anti-Semitism was coined in Germany in the late 19th century to define hatred of Jews, and its meaning remains the same today.)

Reflexively labeling the PIDS anti-Semitic isn't a very successful tactic in public discourse. It fails to address the specifics of their critiques, either by pointing out their lies or by giving context to their distortion of the facts. It also degrades the discussion quite quickly. There is even a term--Godwin's Law-- for this phenomenon when it takes place in online discussion boards and chat rooms: when someone brings in the epithet "Nazi," the discourse quickly decays into playground-level name-calling (though a reasonable exception can be made when actual Nazi symbols are employed, as when Hamas rioters at the Gaza border fence in 2018 flew flags and launched firebomb kites decorated with swastikas). But most importantly, resorting too quickly to the label of "anti-Semite" plays right into the main tactic that PIDS employ to avoid responding to challenges.

There's no need to allow PIDS to deploy this rhetorical "get out of jail free" card. It lets them escape having to defend their arguments on the facts and the merits. It lets them caricature any challenger as an "Israel right or wrong" hyper-partisan. And it allows them to claim that even legitimate criticism of Israel is "muzzled."

Anti-Israel groups often protect themselves from the charge of being anti-Semitic by having anti-Zionist Jews prominently involved in their efforts. Sabeel and American Muslims for Palestine, for instance, both collaborated with Jewish Voice for Peace (the most prominent Jewish-led anti-Zionist organization) in posting transit ads to promote their misrepresentations of history and promote the "one-state final solution." Many members of these "Jewish" groups use their heritage to speak out against Israel "as-a-Jew," which gets media attention for the same reason that a "Man Bites Dog" incident is far more newsworthy than a "Dog Bites Man" event. The practice of using these "as-a-Jew" groups to shield against charges of anti-Semitism has been termed "Jew-washing" by Yitzhak Santis, formerly the director of the Middle East Project at the San Francisco-based Jewish Community Relations Council. [30]

The existence of these anti-Zionist Jews who oppose Israel, not on religious grounds but on philosophical and political positions, has been a matter of extensive discussion within the pro-Israel community. As the Haggadah's parable of the contrary child illustrates, this phenomenon is not new to the Jewish people. From the Biblical era through the darkest times of the Jewish people, there have always been those who side with our enemies. Perhaps this is because they are continuing adolescent rebellion against their parents and community well into adulthood. Perhaps, sadly, they have internalized the anti-Semitism that they have experienced and are trying to prove that they are "good Jews" who don't deserve to be hated along with the rest of us. Some of them cite the opposition to Zionism that was indeed a position held by a significant portion of the European Jewish community in the last century. But that debate within the Jewish community was settled in the killing fields and gas chambers of the Holocaust-- because there was no Jewish state to which they could flee. Whatever their motivation, with

---

[30] http://www.jweekly.com/article/full/60302/anti-israel-protesters-ramp-things-up-locally/

the advent of the internet, the "as-a-Jew" extremists are now able to punch above the weight of their small numbers.

Jewish Voice for Peace, which has openly allied itself with both Christian and Muslim anti-Israel groups, claims to be "agnostic" on the question of Zionism, but its record exposes its true beliefs. This picture is from an anti-Israel pro-Hezbollah rally in San Francisco in August 2006 in which Jewish Voice for Peace participated.

Photo courtesy of zombie of zombietime.com

Now while it's usually counterproductive to label your opponent's statements as anti-Semitism in public discourse, and absolutely wrong to label all criticism of Israel that way, it doesn't mean that there isn't an element of anti-Semitism at work here. Not everyone suffering from Israel Derangement Syndrome is an anti-Semite, but all anti-Semites are PIDS! At the heart of many anti-Israel groups is a dark core of anti-Semitic hatred that has reinvented itself as the more "politically correct" anti-Zionism. As New York Times columnist Thomas Friedman wrote in 2002, "[c]riticizing Israel is not anti-Semitic, and saying so is vile. But singling out Israel for opprobrium and international sanction -- out of all proportion to any other party in the Middle East -- is anti-Semitic, and not saying so is dishonest." Even a casual observer of PIDS must realize that Friedman has just described their playbook.

Of course, anyone expressing support for the Hamas regime can legitimately be charged with anti-Semitism; Hamas has promoted the most bloodthirsty hate speech against Jews since the Holocaust. Their charter quotes this hadith (a saying attributed to Mohammed): "The Day of Judgment will not come about until Muslims fight the Jews (killing the Jews), when the Jew will hide behind stones and trees. The stones and trees will say O Muslims, O Abdulla, there is a Jew behind me, come and kill him." Hamas official TV has broadcast videos with statements such as "Killing Jews is worship that draws us close to Allah" and "We are a nation that drinks blood, and there is no better blood than the blood of Jews." Most of the PIDS will try to distance themselves from Hamas, but recent years have witnessed anti-Israel demonstrators in the Netherlands chanting "Hamas, Hamas, Jews to the gas." In San Francisco, demonstrators have proudly displayed flags of Hamas, Hezbollah (the Lebanese Shiite terror group that worked hard in Syria killing civilians on behalf of the Assad regime), and the PFLP (Popular Front for the Liberation of Palestine) which has conducted airline hijackings and numerous murders of Israeli civilians.

Natan Sharansky, a former Soviet political prisoner who made aliyah after his release and subsequently became a Knesset minister, published a landmark article in 2004 in which he proposed the "3D test" to determine whether criticism of Israel was indeed anti-Semitic: whether it included demonization of Israel, double standards applied to Israel that were not applied to other democratic countries, and delegitimization of Israel. [31]

Demonization involves taking Israel's actions out of any reasonable context or proportion—for example, comparing Israel's actions to those of Nazi Germany, or claiming that Israel is the greatest human rights violator in the world. It also can present as frankly ludicrous accusations, such as Hamas' claim in 2009 that Israel was trying to "destroy" young Gazans by distributing chewing gum laced with aphrodisiac.[32] Double standards are in play when, as noted in the last chapter, the UN focuses a wildly disproportionate amount of resources on condemning Israel while ignoring human rights violations on a massive scale across the Arab world. Double standards are demonstrated when even "pro-Palestinian" groups remain silent while the Assad regime in Syria puts the Palestinian refugees in Yarmouk under a brutal and horrific siege, yet when Hamas fighters try to invade Israel and are killed in the process, their Twitter accounts explode with righteous rage. Likewise, the world remains silent about Turkey's ongoing occupation of northern Cyprus, or its repeated attacks on Kurdish civilians in Syria. On the other hand, you have to be living entirely off the

---

[31] http://www.jcpa.org/phas/phas-sharansky-f04.htm

[32] https://www.ynetnews.com/articles/0,7340,L-3746017,00.html

grid to be unaware of Israel's presence in the West Bank. Certainly you'd also have to consider the open discussion, in otherwise polite society, of whether Israel's existence as a country should even be tolerated, while rogue regimes that oppress their own people and threaten their neighbors, such as North Korea or Iran, are not considered for elimination as nations. Delegitimization, which is the core strategy of any of the groups in which PIDS join together, denies the right of the Jewish people—and only the Jewish people—to national self-determination in part of our ancient homeland. That's the meaning of anti-Zionism. Some of the PIDS will state that they don't agree with the concept of nation-states or religion at all, but their list of nations to be eliminated always seems to start ---and end-- with the Jewish one.

To Sharansky's list we can add a fourth D: "damned if you do, damned if you don't." (Hat tip to Yosef Kutner – @ynkutner on Twitter—for this idea). This is criticism of Israel for not acting as *badly* as other countries routinely do under similar circumstances. For example, Hen Mazzig (an Israeli who spent several years in the US working as an educator for StandWithUs) relates the following story: "A professor asked me if I knew how many Palestinians have been raped by IDF forces. I answered that as far as I knew, none. She triumphantly responded that I was right, because, she said, 'You IDF soldiers don't rape Palestinians because Israelis are so racist and disgusted by them that you won't touch them.'"[33] Yes, you read that correctly—the IDF was being condemned for NOT raping Palestinian women. Similarly, Israel was criticized in 2012 when internal documents were released showing calculations meant to ensure that

---

[33] http://blogs.timesofisrael.com/an-israeli-soldiers-call-to-american-jews/

enough food aid was being delivered to Gaza to avoid malnutrition--while Hamas was busy firing rockets at Israel from Gaza. These were, of course, falsely portrayed by the PIDS as limiting the amount of food that Israel permitted to enter Gaza. Even when Israel does something good, the 4th D comes into play. Because PIDS can't say anything good about Israel, they have to dismiss anything positive as not being genuine. In 2011, a radical academic named Sarah Schulman (PIDS category: anti-Zionist Jews) condemned promotion of Israel's achievements in LGBTQ rights as "pinkwashing," "a deliberate strategy to conceal the continuing violations of Palestinians' human rights behind an image of modernity signified by Israeli gay life." [34] Of course, while Schulman goes to great lengths to avoid criticizing Arab states for their persecution of LGBTQ individuals, I'm sure she'd be leading the charge against Israel if it followed similar policies.

All this gives credence to the quip by British MP Michael Gove: "Antizionism is not a brave anti-colonial stance, it is simply antisemitism minding its manners so it can sit in a seminar room."

Now of course those who engage in this type of criticism will hotly deny that they are anti-Semitic. But then again, aside from genuine Nazis, members of Hamas, or Mel Gibson, when was the last time you heard someone actually admit in public to hatred of Jews? Many PIDS have realized that they can catch more flies with baklava than with acidic hatred, and they try to couch their public language in terms of "human rights."

---

[34] https://www.nytimes.com/2011/11/23/opinion/pinkwashing-and-israels-use-of-gays-as-a-messaging-tool.html

Sometimes the hate still gets the best of them, as well chronicled by photographers such as the Bay Area's Zombie (www.zombietime.com), and as seen in footage of anti-Israel demonstrations during Israel's Operation Pillar of Defense in 2012 (calling Israel supporters "Zionist scum"[35] and dropping an "F*** you, Jew" against Israel supporters [36]). PIDS will also frequently resort to old anti-Semitic tropes recycled for modern consumption—charges that Israel poisons the water supply of Palestinians echo the medieval charge that Jews poisoned wells resulting in disease, and the medieval blood libels of "child-killer" are now hurled against college students who dare to stand up for Israel. What they say on social media (when they think people aren't looking) is both revealing and shocking. Organizations such as Canary Mission in the US, and researchers such as David Collier in the UK, have found posts from anti-Israel activists denying the Holocaust (while, in a remarkable feat of cognitive dissonance, simultaneously praising Hitler) and posting about conspiracies involving the Rothschilds.

Despite their underlying hatred, many PIDS have realized that using the language of "itbach el yahud" (Arabic for "kill the Jew") doesn't work well on campus or with church groups. That's why, in polite company, they prefer to speak about "human rights" while denying the rights of Israeli citizens to live free from terror attacks, and creating their own version of "international law" to condemn Israel's attempts to defend itself.

<hr>

[35] http://www.youtube.com/watch?v=VAzbW17NScc

[36] http://www.youtube.com/watch?v=_DrTeFBu1kU

Photo courtesy of zombie of zombietime.com Poster from "anti-war" rally in San Francisco, 2003. (It's not really anti-Semitic, just anti-Israel. Right.)

Yet sometimes, they can't stop themselves from revealing their true colors. In September 2012, Greta Berlin, a co-founder of the Free Gaza Movement, which has organized flotillas to attempt to bring expired medications (as well as political support and Turkish jihadi wannabes) to the Hamas regime in Gaza, posted a link to a video from a notorious British Holocaust denier on the FGM Twitter feed. She had also posted a link to a 1943 Nazi propaganda film on her Facebook page. (Of course, she has personally received a medal from Ismail Haniyeh, the political leader of Hamas in Gaza, so this really shouldn't have been such a surprise.) In the subsequent controversy, many anti-Israel activists sought to distance themselves from both Berlin and the Free Gaza Movement. Some individuals and groups claimed, without the slightest trace of irony, that they were resolutely opposed to all forms of racism-- including anti-Semitism and Zionism. (Yep, they were promoting the "Zionism is racism" trope that even the UN had discarded in shame in 1991.) But some PIDS still openly sided with Berlin and supported one of the many different excuses that she proffered to explain her actions (including the mutually exclusive excuses that she was in a hurry to go to the airport so she didn't check what she was forwarding, and that her account was hacked.)

In August 2015, the Jewish American musician Matisyahu was "disinvited" from the Rototom Sunsplash music festival in Spain under pressure from local BDS activists, after he refused to issue a statement endorsing "Palestinian rights." No other musicians were asked to make political statements in order to perform. After a worldwide outcry, including condemnation from the Spanish government, the festival apologized and reinstated Matisyahu.

The British blogger David Collier, in a February 2017 post, exposed the pervasive presence of Holocaust denial and anti-Semitism within the UK's Palestine Solidarity Campaign.[37] He then released a report in March 2018 which revealed that prominent British anti-Israel politicians, including Labour party

---

[37] http://david-collier.com/psc-riddled-antisemitism/

leader Jeremy Corbyn, had been members of Facebook groups in which such materials were routinely shared with approving comments.[38] All of which goes to show that you can take the PIDS out of the black hole of hate, but you can't take the black hole of hate out of the PIDS.

The US State Department, in its 2004 report on global anti-Semitism, noted "[t]he demonization of Israel, or vilification of Israeli leaders, sometimes through comparisons with Nazi leaders, and through the use of Nazi symbols to caricature them, indicates an anti-Semitic bias rather than a valid criticism of policy concerning a controversial issue."[39] This often presents as "Holocaust inversion"—minimizing the uniqueness of the industrial-scope murder of millions of Jews simply for being Jews, while conflating the (mostly self-inflicted) situation of the Palestinians into the "human rights" issue that draws attention and resources away from those who are genuinely being oppressed around the globe. It leads to obscenities such as posters of Anne Frank in a keffiyeh, or a photo of concentration camp survivors holding signs saying "Free Palestine." The comparison sometimes takes the form of "You, of all people, should know better than to act in this way." Sadly, we do know quite a few lessons from history—we know how the world refused to allow us any place to flee when faced with imminent genocide. We know how the British caved in to the Mufti and his terror gangs, and closed the door of the Jewish homeland to Jewish refugees. We know how the world community, through the United Nations, continues to provide a

---

[38] http://david-collier.com/exclusive-corbyn-antisemitism/

[39] http://www.state.gov/j/drl/rls/40258.htm

platform for demonization of Israel. What we, as a people, have indeed learned is that we cannot rely on others to guarantee our safety or our survival.

photo by the author. Israel hater protesting in San Francisco June 2012. Note the sign: "What Germany did to the Jews, Israel is doing to the Palestinians."

Staying away from charging your opponent with anti-Semitism doesn't mean that you can't allow others to draw their own conclusions. Ask the PIDS to explain why a Jewish state is unacceptable when dozens of nations declare themselves to be Islamic states.

Member States of the Organization of Islamic Cooperation

Afghanistan	Guyana	Pakistan
Albania	Indonesia	Palestine
Algeria	Iran	Qatar
Azerbaijan	Iraq	Saudi Arabia
Bahrain	Jordan	Senegal
Bangladesh	Kazakhstan	Sierra Leone
Benin	Kuwait	Somalia
Brunei-Darussalam	Kyrgyz Republic	Sudan
Burkina-Faso	Lebanon	Suriname
Cameroon	Libya	Syrian Arab Republic*
Chad	Malaysia	Tajikistan
Comoros	Maldives	Togo
Cote d'Ivoire	Mali	Tunisia
Djibouti	Mauritania	Turkey
Egypt	Morocco	Turkmenistan
Gabon	Mozambique	Uganda
Gambia	Niger	United Arab Emirates
Guinea	Nigeria	Uzbekistan
Guinea-Bissau	Oman	Yemen

*Syria was suspended from the OIC on August 15, 2012 for the government's violent suppression of the revolt in the country.

By comparison, the list of members of the (fictional) "Organization of Jewish States" is comprised of:

Israel.

Ask the PIDS why Gaza, whose population has grown 64% from 2000 to 2017, and where the infant mortality rate is lower than that of Turkey or Brazil), is "just like the Warsaw Ghetto."

Photo by Emad Nassar/Flash 90

A food store in Gaza, 2014. (Just like the Warsaw Ghetto?)

Remind your opponents that the Arab population of the West Bank has more than tripled since Israel took over the territory in 1967. Ask them exactly what they refer to when they say "what Germany did to the Jews, Israel is doing to the Palestinians." And as they try to backpedal away from those ridiculous assertions (or dig themselves a deeper hole by trying to justify them), reasonable people will be able to see through their veneer of "human rights advocacy."

Key points:

Don't be quick to charge PIDS with anti-Semitism. Not all criticism of Israel is anti-Semitic, but that doesn't mean that none of it is. Know how to recognize the "3D" (or "4D") signs.

Challenge the PIDS on their hyperbole about Israel.

Chapter 10: BDS—It's Not Just A Fetish

If you walk through a busy square in Cambridge or Boston or San Francisco at rush hour, at some point you're sure to see a group of wrinkly Israel haters passing out photos of broken Palestinian children which (via a syllogism known only to the BDSers) means you should stop buying hummus made in Massachusetts or New Jersey. -- http://divestthis.com/2011/06/be-with-us.html

"BDS" sounds like something that should be a heading in the "personals" section of your local alternative weekly newspaper. It's actually the rubric under which the PIDS bring their program of lies and hate to university campuses, convocations of Protestant church denominations, and deliberations of local governments.

BDS stands for "boycott, divestment and sanctions" against Israel. And like every other activity of the PIDS, these are tactics to be utilized not in the name of peace between a Jewish state of Israel and an Arab state of Palestine, but against Israel's very existence. A more appropriate description of their movement would be "Bully, Defame and Slander."

The BDS movement originated at the infamous "United Nations Conference against Racism" in Durban, South Africa in September 2001. This meeting was notable for a parallel conference of non-governmental organizations (NGO's) which conducted anti-Israel demonstrations and issued a statement labeling Israel a "racist apartheid state." That document also called for a program of boycotts of Israeli goods and companies doing business with Israel; divestment by churches, universities and governments from companies doing business with Israel; and international sanctions against Israel. These were directed not at Israel's presence in Judea and Samaria (and, at the time, Gaza), but at all of Israel.

(Poster circulated at the Durban NGO conference in 2001.)

In 2004, Palestinian groups built on this foundation of hate by issuing a call for an academic and cultural boycott of Israel, followed in 2005 by a call for a comprehensive BDS program against Israel. The latter document had 3 demands issued against Israel:

"1. Ending its occupation and colonization of all Arab lands and dismantling the Wall;

2. Recognizing the fundamental rights of the Arab-Palestinian citizens of Israel to full equality; and

3. Respecting, protecting and promoting the rights of Palestinian refugees to return to their homes and properties as stipulated in UN resolution 194."[40]

The first one is, no doubt deliberately, vague. Exactly what constitutes "Arab lands?" Is it just the West Bank and Gaza, or is it all of Israel? After all, the Hamas charter states "[t]he Islamic Resistance Movement believes that the land of Palestine is an Islamic Waqf (religious endowment) consecrated for future Muslim generations until Judgment Day. It, or any part of it, should not be squandered: it, or any part of it, should not be given up." And who is the first group listed on their website in support of this BDS Call? The "Council of National and Islamic Forces in Palestine (Coordinating body for the major political parties in the Occupied Palestinian Territory)," which includes the terror groups Hamas, Popular Front for the Liberation of Palestine and Palestinian Islamic Jihad. This Council is probably a more politically influential group than the dozens of other NGO's listed, most of which (the Union of Palestinian Farmers, for instance) probably aren't more than a mailbox at Ramallah's equivalent of the UPS Store.

The second demand—for full equality for Palestinian citizens of Israel (in other words, Israeli Arabs)—is not unreasonable on its face. But again the wording is deliberately vague—what type of equality? Israeli Arab citizens have the right to vote, they have civil rights, and they have the right to

---

[40] http://www.bdsmovement.net/call

petition the courts to uphold those rights. Should the 25% of Israel's population that is Arab be granted an equal say in the country's decisions as the 75% that is Jewish? Should an Arab's vote be worth three times that of a Jew's? Wouldn't that be, instead, unequal? (Actually, that is exactly what some Arab leaders have demanded. In a 2006, document entitled "The Future Vision of the Palestinian Arabs in Israel", the National Committee for the Heads of the Arab Local Authorities in Israel demanded political reforms that would give the Arab minority a political veto.[41])

Can Israel's Arab towns receive better funding, and can their socioeconomic status be improved? Can steps be taken to end the racism that exists in Israel (as it does in every country in the world)? Of course. But given the situation of Arabs across the Middle East, an Arab citizen of Israel has far more rights and is far better off economically than most of her fellow Arabs, in addition to not being subjected to legally excused honor killings and female genital mutilation.

Finally, of course, we get to the heart of the issue, the non-existent "right" of return for the *refugees*. Here the BDS movement gives up any pretense that its goal is peaceful coexistence; it's just another tactic in their ongoing refusal to accept the existence of the Jewish state. This is where BDSers are exposed as PIDS simply hiding behind a slightly different set of letters—essentially, it's the same old b.s. (hold the d). It's the Hamas "river to the sea" agenda dressed up in fancier language. In their campaigns for university and corporate divestment, or public calls for boycotts of Israel, they won't admit that their end

---

[41] http://reut-institute.org/data/uploads/PDFVer/ENG.pdf

goal is the same as that of Hamas and Iran—the elimination of Israel from the map. But even Norman Finkelstein, a dedicated anti-Israel activist with years of controversial statements on his resume (see Chapter Eleven), called out the BDS movement for its duplicity in a 2012 interview circulated widely on YouTube:

"I'm not going to tolerate what I think is silliness, childishness, and a lot of leftist posturing. I mean we have to be honest, and I loathe the disingenuous. They don't want Israel. They think they are being very clever; they call it their three-tier. We want the end of the occupation, we want the right of return, and we want equal rights for Arabs in Israel. And they think they are very clever because they know the result of implementing all three is what, what's the result?

You know and I know what's the result. There's no Israel!

...

They're talking about they want to destroy Israel. And in fact I think they're right, I think that's true. I'm not going to lie. But this kind of duplicity and disingenuous, "oh we're agnostic about Israel." No you're not agnostic! You don't want it!

... You talk about BDS, they make all these claims about their victories. All their claims about their victories. You know what? You see these ten fingers? These more than suffice to count all their victories. There are superfluous fingers here to count all their victories. It's a cult! Where the guru says 'we have all these victories' and everyone nods their head and no one sits down to do the arithmetic on their own. Yes, it's had some victories; no question about it. But the way people promote it as if it's proven itself and we're on the verge of a victory of some sort. It's just sheer nonsense. It's sheer nonsense. It's a cult. And I personally am tired of it."[42]

It's very telling that there is not a single organization in the United States that supports BDS that also supports peace between the Jewish state of Israel and its neighbors. Not one. And, conversely, there is not a single group supporting Israel's existence as a Jewish state that supports BDS. Even the most left-wing pro-Israel groups-- Ameinu, Americans for Peace Now, and J Street—all explicitly reject BDS.

BDS advocates will sometimes claim that supporting BDS isn't anti-Israel. Either they're so intellectually lazy that they haven't even read their own leaders' statements, or they're assuming that their listeners will be too uninformed to be able to counter that deception (good thing you're reading this book, isn't it?).

BDS leaders have a lengthy track record of making their intentions quite clear. Here are just a few quotes from prominent BDS activists (these and many more can be found here: http://www.jewishvirtuallibrary.org/bds-in-their-own-words).

From Omar Barghouti, one of the co-founders of PACBI, the Palestinian Campaign for the Academic and Cultural Boycott of Israel:

"Going back to the two-state solution, besides having passed its expiry date, it was never a moral solution to start with."

"Definitely, most definitely we oppose a Jewish state in any part of Palestine."

Lara Kiswani, who heads the San Francisco-based Arab Resource and Organizing Center, which promotes BDS, is very clear on her goals: "Bringing down Israel will really benefit everyone in the world and everyone in society." Or as Anna Balzer, a BDS activist, put it more succinctly: "We need to wipe out Israel."

The US Campaign for the Academic and Cultural Boycott of Israel, a leading BDS organization, isn't hesitant to declare its official policy—or to use imagery that gives a wink and a nod to violence.

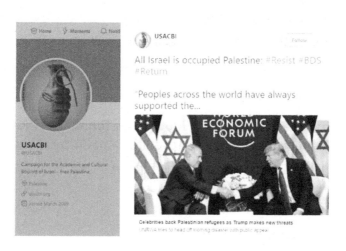

Sometimes BDS leaders allow the mask to slip in even more spectacular fashion. When the student government at UC Davis passed a divestment resolution in January 2015 (which of course the university administration immediately announced would not be implemented), one of the student government sponsors of the resolution posted this picture on her Facebook page, proudly claiming that "Hamas and Sharia law have taken over UC Davis."

(I'm glad nobody informed the campus police, who would then have been required to force women to wear burkas.)

It should therefore come as no surprise that the leading US BDS organization, the US Campaign for Palestinian Rights (note, once again, how the most important "Palestinian right" is the right to eliminate the Jewish state) was exposed in 2018 as having funneled US tax-deductible donations to the West Bank and Gaza-based BDS National Committee, which is linked to

Hamas and other terror organizations via the aforementioned Council for National and Islamic Forces in Palestine.[43]

The BDS movement has had a long track record of failure in the United States. Not one American college or university has adopted a policy that, on political grounds, restricts investments in Israeli companies or in companies doing business with Israel. While a small food co-op in Olympia Washington did indeed override its own rules of procedure to institute a boycott of Israeli goods, other co-ops around the country (most notably the large Park Slope Food Co-Op in Brooklyn in 2012) failed to adopt BDS proposals. On several occasions when BDS proposals have come to a public vote (in Seattle WA and Somerville MA) they have been roundly defeated despite strong efforts by PIDS.

These strong efforts by BDS activists include acts of vandalism and harassment against those who dare to defy their edicts. In California, BDS activists went to several Trader Joe's stores (which carry Israeli products, including couscous and packaged frozen cubes of garlic, basil and cilantro) and vandalized the Israeli products there, and in at least one store started a fire in a trash can. A variety store in San Francisco has been repeatedly invaded by BDSers who block the aisles because it refuses to acquiesce to their demand that it stop selling Israeli goods. And any musician who plans to perform in Israel can count on the BDS outrage machine to orchestrate a multitude of hate messages on their Facebook page by "fans," many of whom had never heard of the performer until plans to perform in Israel were announced, or by progressives who

---

[43]   http://www.thetower.org/6322-tablet-magazine-anti-israel-boycott-group-has-financial-ties-to-terror-groups/

somehow failed to be infuriated by the performer's previous concerts in human rights paradises such as Russia, China or Lebanon. Paul McCartney (who EVERYONE has heard of) reported receiving death threats, as did members of the Argentine soccer team which caused them to cancel a match in Israel in 2018. (So much for the claims that BDS is "non-violent" activism.)

The BDS movement has not been averse to declaring "victories" that were quickly discovered to be fraudulent. In February 2009, the BDS movement proudly trumpeted on its website that "Hampshire College in Amherst, MA, has become the first of any college or university in the U.S. to divest from companies on the grounds of their involvement in the Israeli occupation of Palestine. This landmark move is a direct result of a two-year intensive campaign by the campus group, Students for Justice in Palestine (SJP)." Within days, the Hampshire's president publicly noted that the college had not in fact divested from Israel, and that although it had sold shares of companies targeted by SJP, that sale was in no way related to Israel, and that Hampshire continued to hold millions of dollars in investments in Israeli companies and companies doing business with Israel.

BDS activists attempted to repeat the same fraud in August 2010 when they claimed that Harvard University had divested from Israel. This time the hoax was corrected within hours, when Harvard pointed out that since Israel had just been admitted to the Organization for Economic Co-operation and Development (the club of the world's economically advanced countries) it was no longer considered an "emerging economy," which meant that Harvard had to sell shares of Israeli companies in that sector of its massive portfolio.

More recently in 2012, the large mutual fund investment group TIAA-CREF sold shares of Caterpillar Corporation (CAT) from one of its many mutual funds, the Socially Responsible Fund, because Caterpillar had been delisted from the companies on the index used by TIAA-CREF. Never mind that TIAA-CREF still held millions of dollars in CAT stock in its other portfolios, and never mind that TIAA-CREF's response to the BDS groups over the past two years had been the polite corporate version of "get lost," and never mind that the decision to delist CAT was made by an independent third party, MSCI, and never mind that the decision was made primarily because of CAT's labor relations and closure of a large plant in Canada related to labor issues there. Oh—and never mind that CAT has dealerships in both Ramallah and Gaza, because the Palestinians aren't boycotting CAT. BDS activists jumped on this news as proof that their efforts had caused TIAA-CREF to divest itself of CAT stock, and promptly called on their supporters to rally outside TIAA-CREF's New York offices to.... urge them to divest from CAT! (Wait, didn't they say that they had already won that battle?)

The standard BDS Kabuki theater plays itself out on a small number of campuses every year, and its script is highly predictable. First, get BDS advocates elected to the student government without them admitting that they intend to subject their campus to a divisive and controversial debate. Second, design a resolution ostensibly about "universal human rights" but ensure that the only country mentioned is Israel. Israeli companies will not necessarily be targeted, but rather companies that work with Israel to help with matters such as defense and security. Third, schedule the debate with as little notice as possible to the Jewish community on campus; if at all possible, schedule it on the Jewish High Holidays or Passover, so that many Jewish students will be off campus or observing the holiday. (The short notice will almost always be a violation of the student government's own rules of procedure, but the BDS mantra in such cases is that such rules never apply to them.) Fourth, show up en masse with "intersectional" allies and sit together; try to intimidate any pro-Israel student especially by jeering and snickering. Fifth, select speakers from the Vladimir Lenin school of speechmaking—delivering the speech in a shout, with raised fists in the air is *de rigeur*. Finally, if victorious, BDS advocates will break into chants of "allah hu ackbar." If defeated, they will place duct tape over mouths to indicate that they have been "silenced" (after an hours-long debate in the student government), and sometimes even physically confront the student government representatives who dared to vote against them. During and after this process, Jewish students on campus will be subjected to harassment and swastikas may be painted on the campus Hillel center or Jewish fraternity. The university president will quickly announce that the school will not be divesting from these companies. The student government itself may even investigate the violations of conduct by the BDS proponents. Wash, rinse, and repeat next year.

It's not just the students who hijack their organizations in support of BDS' bigotry. Faculty in the social sciences and humanities often demand the same of their own academic organizations. In 2013, the American Studies Association adopted a boycott of Israeli academics. Its president at the time, Curtis Marez of the University of California at San Diego, was asked why of all the countries in the world with far worse human rights violations the ASA chose to single out Israel. He famously answered "One has to start somewhere," echoing what many tyrants across the centuries have likely said about the Jews. To the surprise of absolutely nobody, the ASA also chose the exact same point to conclude its comprehensive crusade for human rights. Subsequently, emails surfaced showing that pro-BDS leaders of the ASA conspired to hide their agenda when running for their leadership positions, and violated the organization's own procedural rules to get their boycott passed; they are now being sued in Federal court.

(Interestingly, faculty in the physical science, biology and engineering departments are much less represented in BDS activities. Perhaps that's because science relies on observable facts and has an established methodology to weed out incorrect theories. So while Judith Butler, a professor of literature at UC Berkeley, can claim that Hamas and Hezbollah are progressive movements, the same level of asininity from an engineer will result in a billion-dollar bridge falling into a bay.)

Although BDS has spectacularly failed to gain traction in the United States, this hasn't deterred them from proclaiming every failure as a "victory" in one form or another. (Somebody should tell them that BDS votes are not like golf, where the low score wins.)

Even when BDS does win, Palestinians lose. One of the prime targets of the BDS movement in recent years has been the Sodastream company, which was located across the 1949 armistice line, and employed both Jews and Arabs. Palestinian workers from the West Bank were paid at Israeli wages, which was far more than they could earn in the Palestinian economy. BDS relentlessly targeted Sodastream, which was the largest private employer of Palestinians in the world, and the company has now moved its factory to Israel's Negev desert. As a result, hundreds of Palestinian workers lost their well-paying jobs. Yet Omar Barghouti, one of the leaders of the BDS movement, expressed no concern for the hundreds of Palestinian families whose livelihoods were affected. To Barghouti, this was a "clear-cut victory."[44]

One of the few arenas in which BDS has had partial success is with some of the American Protestant churches. In 2004 the Presbyterian Church-USA voted to endorse divestment from Israel, via a resolution pushed through by a small group of PIDS within the Church. The subsequent outcry from the general membership resulted in this being overturned at their next General Assembly in 2006 and their refusal to adopt such a resolution in 2012. They did narrowly adopt such a resolution in 2014, but to get it passed also required the resolution to disavow the goals of the BDS movement by supporting a two state solution.

The United Methodist Church also refused to endorse a divestment resolution brought by BDS activists in 2012, but in 2014 it did vote to sell $110,000 worth of investments in a British security company that sold equipment to Israel.

These small, symbolic victories for BDSers came in what was truly a rigged game. The radical Palestinian Christian anti-Israel group Sabeel was able to represent the "Palestinian cause" in these assemblies, and the activists who were setting the rules for these "debates" chose, as a representative of the Jewish community, the radical fringe anti-Israel group Jewish Voice for Peace. This tactic is often used in church events about Israel—"balancing" the anti-Israel Christian viewpoint with an anti-Israel Jewish one. Israel advocates, and people of goodwill

---

[44] http://nypost.com/2015/09/13/the-price-palestinians-pay-for-bds-victory/

in both Jewish and Christian communities who value interfaith cooperation, need to continue pushing back against this tactic. Fortunately, there are many such people doing so within these churches, such as Presbyterians for Middle East Peace.

Ultimately, the goal of the BDS movement is not actually to cause harm to the Israeli economy by enacting boycotts or divestment measures. Israel's spectacular growth in GDP, its growing business ties around the world, and its steady increase in tourism since the launch of BDS in 2001 are testament to the impossibility of that task. Rather, the goal of the BDS Movement is to continue to proffer the same lies and distortions year after year, to slowly poison the minds of students on campus and the public, and to harm Israel's image. By ruthlessly bullying those genuinely interested in dialogue and coexistence, they hope to dominate the conversation with their extreme position. BDS advocates are constantly trying to get legitimate organizations to sign on to any part of their agenda (or to lie that they have done so). They will then market that support to other groups as a complete endorsement of the entire BDS program and urge them to take a similarly "moral" stance. That's why they are quick to jump on anything resembling a boycott or a divestment so they can (mis)use the good name of a university, an investment house, or your child's co-op preschool as a supporter of their "river-to-the-sea" program.

When an organization allows BDS in, there isn't a warning label about the nasty side effects that may occur: internal discord, recriminations, and even lawsuits. As the New York Times reported about the Park Slope Food Coop, "[t]he debate has splintered the membership, turned neighbor against neighbor and provoked threats of litigation." When the 2010 UC Berkeley divestment resolution was vetoed by the student government president, he specifically noted "[t]o achieve and maintain campus unity and peace, the perception of the bill as a symbolic attack on a specific community of our fellow students, and/or fears of the bill being used as a tool to delegitimize the state of Israel, cannot be overstated." And, as Eylon Aslan-Levy noted in the Times of Israel in February 2014, "no society has ever worked out how to demonise half the world's Jewish population without demonising the other half too."[45]

(While there was a vote by the Durham, NC City Council in April of 2018 to ban any police trainings in Israel, this was not a vote endorsing the BDS agenda. Nonetheless, the demonization and divisiveness on display during this episode was held in the same kangaroo-court atmosphere we see on campuses. In this case, the vote was not even to change anything currently in effect, because Durham had never had, nor planned, to have, any such trainings.)

The tragedy that the Palestinian leadership created for its own people was choosing to forego the opportunity for the first ever Palestinian state, in the interests of preventing the Jewish people from enjoying the same sovereignty. As we saw in Chapter Three, they made that mistake during the period of the British Mandate, rejecting proposals in 1937 and 1947 for independent Arab and Jewish states. Arafat then doubled down on this bad bet in 2000 by not only rejecting the proposal at Camp David, but also launching the terror war that lasted for the next five years and cost the lives of thousands. BDS is simply another means to the same end, utilizing different weapons towards the same goal. Just as the decisions made by the Palestinian leadership over the decades have prolonged rather

---

[45] http://blogs.timesofisrael.com/if-the-bds-wins-the-jews-are-next/

than resolved the conflict (and their own stateless situation), BDS will end up doing the same both by framing the conflict as a zero-sum game and by prioritizing the elimination of the Jewish state over the creation of a Palestinian Arab one.

In medieval folklore, the vampires can't enter your home unless you invite them in. Make sure that BDS doesn't get invited into your own community-- once the BDS circus has moved on, to use your organization's "endorsement" somewhere else, they're not going to deal with the rancor and chaos that is invariably left in their wake. But if BDS does indeed darken the door of your college, your food co-op, or your community, you can educate your fellow citizens about the BDS track record. Most of all, you can talk about the one thing that is the garlic to the BDS vampire: peace between a Jewish state of Israel and the Palestinians.

Key points:

Don't let BDSers present themselves as pro- peace.

Expose the real goals of the BDS movement.

Chapter 11: Exposing Their "Experts"

Where are the clowns? Send in the clowns. Don't bother, they're here.- Stephen Sondheim, "Send in the Clowns"

Some of Israel's most vicious opponents have provided us with a veritable treasure trove of nonsensical statements on Israel as well as other subjects. PIDS will have a difficult time defending these figures as authoritative once you are able to "out, name and shame" them.

Omar Barghouti: Barghouti, born in Qatar and raised in Egypt, is one of the co-founders of PACBI, the Palestinian Campaign for the Academic and Cultural Boycott of Israel. He travels across the US and Europe urging universities to boycott Israeli institutions and divest from Israel. Yet Barghouti was also a graduate student for many years—at Tel Aviv University! When asked why he studies at a university against which he proposes boycotts, he has replied "My studies are a personal matter and I have no interest in commenting."[46] I'm guessing that Barghouti failed to study history when he was at TAU: "[Jews] did not suffer in Arab countries. There were no pogroms. There was no persecution."[47]

Ilan Pappé: Pappé, an ex-Israeli, is a professor at the University of Exeter and an avowed Marxist. His book The Ethnic Cleansing of Palestine is frequently cited by PIDS and has been heavily criticized by even leftist Israelis such as the historian Benny Morris. At least Pappé is honest about his "scholarship:" "Indeed the struggle is about ideology, not about facts. Who knows what facts are? We try to convince as many people as we can that our interpretation of the facts is the correct one, and we do it because of ideological reasons, not because we are truthseekers."[48]

"The debate between us is on one level between historians who believe they are purely objective reconstructers of the past, like [Benny] Morris, and those who claim that they are subjective human beings striving to tell their own version of the past, like myself."[49]

---

[46] http://www.camera.org/index.asp?x_context=7&x_issue=51&x_article=1803

[47] https://www.ynetnews.com/articles/0,7340,L-4679117,00.html

[48] "An Interview of Ilan Pappé," Baudouin Loos, Le Soir [Bruxelles],Nov. 29, 1999

[49] "Benny Morris's Lies About My Book," Ilan Pappé, Response to Morris' critique of Pappé's book, A History of Palestine, published in the New Republic, March 22, 2004, History News Network, April 5, 2004

Those are rather remarkable admissions for someone who claims to be a "historian." I just hope he doesn't take the same view of traffic laws when he drives. "Really, officer, my version is that this parked car hit my vehicle; that fits my ideology better."

Pappé had also claimed, during the runup to the 2003 US invasion of Iraq, that the Israelis were going to take advantage of the war to expel the Palestinians en masse from the West Bank.

At least if he's wrong, he's consistently wrong.

Ali Abunimah: Abunimah is a Palestinian-American, co-founder of the cheerily named "Electronic Intifada" website (a title which makes you wonder if it will make your computer explode in your face). His 2006 book, <u>One Country: A Bold Proposal to End the Israeli-Palestinian Conflict</u>, promotes the One-State Final Solution discussed in Chapter Seven. To this end, he supports Hamas taking over the West Bank "to engage [it] in the resistance project." (Which presumably includes placing rocket launchers near apartments and playgrounds, to help create more "martyrs" when Israel defends itself.) Abunimah has consistently been a cheerleader for the most extreme position among the Palestinian factions, with statements such as "'Hamas: We will never recognize the enemy.' Let's hope they keep their word."[50]

As noted by the insightful Petra Marquardt-Bigman (who is published in the Times of Israel and Forward.com as well as

---

[50] http://warped-mirror.com/2012/12/10/donate-for-a-daily-dose-of-hate/

at her own warped-mirror.com), "As hard as Abunimah may try to pose as a progressive anti-racist and defender of human rights, his enthusiastic cheerleading for Hamas and groups like Islamic Jihad ultimately means going along with the seething Jew-hatred expressed in the Hamas Charter and in countless jihadi pronouncements."[51]

In an act combining extreme hubris with awe-inspiring levels of irony, Abunimah has now taken upon himself the role of a fighter against anti-Semitism. He opined on Twitter: "Making Yom Kippur a UN holiday to honor the genocidal 'state' of Israel would be sure way to increase global anti-Jewish sentiment." (Leading one wag to appropriately retort that this sounded just like "Nice synagogue you have here. Would hate to see anything happen to it.")

Richard Falk: Falk, whom we met in Chapter Eight, holds the title of Professor Emeritus of International Law at Princeton University. (That sounds like an impeccable credential, right? But Princeton is now probably quite embarrassed that he can include that on his resume.) In 2008, the United Nations Human Rights Council (UNHRC) appointed Falk to a six-year term as a United Nations Special Rapporteur on "the situation of human rights in the Palestinian territories occupied since 1967." Falk came into that role with an established track record of audacious misjudgment: in a 1979 Op-Ed published in the New York Times, he argued that Iran's Ayatollah Khomeini would provide "a desperately-needed model of humane governance

---

[51] http://warped-mirror.com/2012/12/08/ali-abunimah-hopes-obama-will-make-history-updated/

for a third-world country."[52] (I'm sure that the Iranian victims of torture and public hangings have appreciated such "humane governance" in the years since.)

While serving in the UN, Falk was condemned by UN Secretary-General Ban Ki-Moon for promoting theories that the September 11, 2001 attacks on the US were an inside job. Falk wrote the preface to a book by noted 9/11 conspiracy theorist David Ray Griffin and has promoted these theories on his blog and in the media. Given such a track record, it's not surprising that his 2008 statement that Israel was planning a "Palestinian Holocaust" proved to be just as reliable.

Even the Palestinian Authority called for Falk's resignation in 2010, and Falk admitted that this was because the PA leadership considered him "a partisan of Hamas."[53] Falk apparently tried to reinforce that reputation by likening Hamas to the resistance fighters against the Nazis.[54]

For extra credit, Falk also endorsed the blatant anti-Semitism of ex-Israeli (and ex-Jew who converted to Christianity) Gilad Atzmon's book "The Wandering Who." Atzmon's book was denounced even by prominent PIDS such as Abunimah and Barghouti, as its pervasive stench of anti-

---

[52] http://online.wsj.com/public/resources/documents/gloview021511.pdf

[53] http://www.maannews.net/eng/ViewDetails.aspx?ID=267176

[54] http://www.algemeiner.com/2013/01/28/un-representative-richard-falk-compares-terror-group-hamas-to-wwii-french-resistance/

Semitism and Holocaust denial was so pronounced that even they couldn't overlook it.

John Mearsheimer: Mearsheimer, a professor of political science at the University of Chicago who also endorsed Atzmon's book, is one of the co-authors of The Israel Lobby and US Foreign Policy, a book which claims that Israel's supporters comprise a monolithic power bloc that has a stranglehold on public debate about Israel, and that anyone who dares suggest otherwise is silenced. (Of course, the book reached the New York Times bestseller list and the authors were feted on the talk show circuit for months, demonstrating how effectively they were "silenced" by the Lobby.) The book also is rife with quotes taken out of context in an attempt to prove, among other things, that Israel deliberately expelled most of the Palestinians who became refugees in 1947-8. Mearsheimer's worldview not only tolerates overt anti-Semitism, it also holds that a nuclear weapon in the hands of the Iranian leadership would bring "stability." In 2012, he claimed "I think there's no question that a nuclear-armed Iran would bring stability to the region, because nuclear weapons are weapons of peace. They're weapons of deterrence. They have hardly any offensive capability at all." [55]

(The Japanese might beg to differ.)

Noam Chomsky: Chomsky is an MIT professor of linguistics (which somehow qualifies him as an expert on foreign affairs). He has a lengthy track record of anti-Israel writing and speeches. He traveled to Lebanon in 2006 where he

---

[55] http://www.pbs.org/newshour/bb/world/july-dec12/iran2_07-09.html

openly expressed support for Hezbollah and stated that the radical group should be allowed to maintain its own private army within Lebanon. (I doubt that the majority of the Lebanese who were not affiliated with Hezbollah appreciated Chomsky's support for the terror gang; they probably had some choice linguistic responses of their own.) Chomsky, born and raised as a Jewish American, somehow managed to overlook both the statement by Hezbollah leader Nasrallah that Jews are "grandsons of apes and pigs" and Nasrallah's endorsement of Iran's "Death to America" slogan.

Norman Finkelstein: Finkelstein is an unemployed ex-lecturer at four different universities where he failed to get tenure. He is one of the darlings of the PIDS because not only is he Jewish, but his parents were also Holocaust survivors. A collection of his statements by the watchdog group CAMERA included Finkelstein calling for solidarity with Hezbollah, and mocking Israel as a "lunatic state," "an insane state," and "a Satanic state" bent on war. He labels Jewish leaders involved in Holocaust restitution "gangsters" and "crooks" and termed the late author and speaker Elie Wiesel "the resident clown of the Holocaust circus." He calls Israelis "Satanic, narcissistic people" and claims Israel committed a "slaughter, a massacre" in Gaza and "wants war, war and war."[56]

He met with leaders of Hezbollah, which is second only to Al Qaeda in the number of civilians it has killed by terror attacks, and subsequently wrote an article called "In Defense of Hezbollah." In it he stated "I don't know much about their

---

[56] https://www.camera.org/article/bbc-s-hardtalk-features-norman-finkelstein-smears-israel/

politics, and anyhow, it's irrelevant." Finkelstein's stature among the PIDS diminished greatly in 2012 after the interview cited in Chapter Ten was posted on YouTube.

Max Blumenthal: Blumenthal has replaced Finkelstein as the bad-boy darling of the PIDS, now that Finkelstein has blown their cover story of a "human rights" effort. Blumenthal, whose previous career as a "journalist" included a stint at the pro-Hezbollah Lebanese newspaper al-Akhbar, joined Ali Abunimah on a speaking tour of the US in 2014. Blumenthal cemented his reputation as the clown prince of the PIDS in November 2014 when he received worldwide attention for chasing a left-wing member of the German Parliament into a bathroom, for daring to cancel a meeting with him. Over the past few years, Max has become a defender of the Assad regime in Syria, which has murdered thousands of Palestinian civilians along with Syrians.

In an October 2013 appearance at the University of Pennsylvania, Blumenthal stated that the Jewish population of Israel would have to "become indigenized, to be a part of the Arab world" by external pressure if necessary. That might be worth discussing—as soon as a modern society emerges across the Arab world that provides equal rights for women, for gays, and for anyone who chooses to practice a different religion. (Never mind the fact that, as already demonstrated, Arabs are not the indigenous population of the Levant. And Jews are.)

"Human Rights" NGOs (non-governmental organizations):

Ideally, groups such as Amnesty International and Human Rights Watch would be unbiased observers who assess all situations based on objective and verifiable standards of human rights. In practice, that's unfortunately not the case.

Whether it's responding to the wishes of their donors or falling prey to the biases of their own staffs, these organizations too often demonstrate double standards, demonization and delegitimization of Israel. This misbehavior within the "human rights community" has been so persistent than an entire organization, NGO Monitor, stays quite busy tracking both the actions of these groups and their sources of funding, seeking to hold them accountable. Many leftist NGOs within Israel (such as Breaking the Silence and B'Tselem) are primarily funded by European governments, with an agenda that aims to influence the Israeli political system. Imagine the response in EU countries if the Israeli government were to fund groups promoting one of the many separatist movements there!

NGO Monitor has a wealth of information about these groups on its website https://www.ngo-monitor.org/. Even a small sample reveals the way in which these organizations misuse their supposedly impartial standing to help promote anti-Israel propaganda.

Human Rights Watch: founded in 1978, its founding chairman Robert Bernstein took to the pages of the New York Times in 2009 to publicly disavow its increasing anti-Israel bias. Bernstein's own words are worth repeating here:

"The Arab and Iranian regimes rule over some 350 million people, and most remain brutal, closed and autocratic, permitting little or no internal dissent. The plight of their citizens who would most benefit from the kind of attention a large and well-financed international human rights organization can provide is being ignored as Human Rights Watch's Middle East division prepares report after report on Israel.

Human Rights Watch has lost critical perspective on a conflict in which Israel has been repeatedly attacked by Hamas and Hezbollah, organizations that go after Israeli citizens and use their own people as human shields. These groups are supported by the government of Iran, which has openly declared its intention not just to destroy Israel but to murder Jews everywhere."[57]

There are numerous examples of HRW's unique approach to Israel. It actively participated in the Durban conference in 2001, at which the BDS movement was born. It was instrumental in the creation of the Goldstone Report, later disavowed by its lead author after the facts of the situation had thoroughly discredited it. Its Israel and Palestine director, Omar Shakir, openly endorses the BDS movement, while its Middle East and North Africa Division head, Sarah Leah Whitson, fundraised in Saudi Arabia with the specific sales pitch that they needed resources to counter pro-Israel groups. Moving up the leadership ladder, HRW executive director Ken Roth was a notable anti-Israel presence on Twitter during 2014's Operation Protective Edge[58], and has whitewashed calls by former Iranian President Ahmedinejad to "wipe Israel off the map," claiming that they were not incitement to genocide.

Amnesty International: founded by Peter Benenson (a British Zionist!), it has also fallen into the ditch of anti-Israel partisanship, tarnishing the Nobel Peace Prize that it received in 1977. Supposedly impartial, it has employed known anti-Israel

---

[57] https://www.nytimes.com/2009/10/20/opinion/20bernstein.html?_r=1

[58] https://www.algemeiner.com/2014/09/02/ken-roth's-twitter-war-against-israel/

activists and BDS supporters. In 2015 AI sponsored (along with a number of BDS-endorsing organizations, including Jewish Voice for Peace) a US speaking tour by Bassem Tamimi. Tamimi is a Palestinian who has called for a third intifada and published a Facebook post claiming that Israelis kidnap Palestinian children to steal their organs; another member of his family, Ahlam Tamimi, was the mastermind of the 2001 bombing of the Sbarro pizzeria in Jerusalem that killed 15 civilians and wounded over 100 others. AI has spoken out in support of the entire Tamimi clan. Not surprisingly, AI also focuses disproportionately on Israel and its reports contain highly inflammatory language, including the demand that Israel (but not Hamas) be charged with war crimes at the International Criminal Court. Amnesty did not disavow its campus clubs at several universities in South Africa which actively participated in "Israel Apartheid Week."

The message you should be sending to these groups is: If you were consumed with righteous outrage when dozens of Hamas terrorists were killed trying to invade Israel, and shrug when missiles are indiscriminately fired from Gaza at Israeli towns, then you can stop pretending your outrage is based on morality or human rights.

Key points:

Be prepared when PIDS cite "authorities" who can be exposed as unreliable

When you hear about a supposedly impartial "human rights" organization issuing a report which reads like it was written by card-carrying members of the PIDS, that might just be the case!

Chapter 12: What About Trump?

"There are two kinds of people: those who like Neil Diamond, and those who don't."-- Bill Murray (as Bob Wiley) in "What About Bob?"

In the 1991 dark comedy "What About Bob?" Bill Murray plays Bob, an annoying patient who follows his therapist Leo, played by Richard Dreyfuss, on vacation. Try as he might, Leo just can't get away from Bob.

Similarly, no discussion of advocating for Israel can escape dealing with the phenomenon that is President Donald Trump. Not only is he the president who has been the most openly supportive of Israel, he's also someone who incites strong opinions. You can love him, you can hate him, but there are not many people whose opinion of Trump is "I don't know, meh, I guess." The intensity of public opinion about Trump will affect how those of us in the pro-Israel community respond to actions of his Administration with respect to Israel.

(If you're in the UK, you've got an entirely different problem—you've seen one of your two major parties entirely taken over by the PIDS. So unless you are willing to tolerate a government that will shrug dismissively about anti-Semitism while boycotting Israel, you don't really have a genuine choice in your elections!)

If You're a Trump Supporter:

You're partying in the penthouse suite. Your man is in the White House, and he's done what the pro-Israel community has been asking: recognition of Jerusalem as the capital of Israel; withdrawing from the JCPOA (the nuclear agreement with Iran); signing the Taylor Force Act, thus ending the ability of the Palestinians to receive US aid as long as they continue their "pay-for-slay" terrorist reward program; and cutting US funding of UNRWA because of their role in obstructing peace by perpetuating Palestinian refugee status *ad infinitum*, and teaching Palestinian children "river to the sea" maximalism. He's appointed strong supporters of Israel to key foreign policy positions; you're giving Nikki Haley a standing ovation in your living room for every speech she makes about the Middle East. Everything you hated about President Obama's policies towards Israel is being reversed.

Looking around the world, who is the national leader who is openly closest to Trump? It's Prime Minister Netanyahu.

Israelis love Trump. A May 2018 poll (taken after the US Embassy move and around the time that the withdrawal from the JCPOA was announced) showed 59% of Jewish Israelis held a favorable opinion of him, 19% unfavorable, and rest were, well, "meh" (OK, so there are indeed a few...). Even among secular Israelis, 45% held a favorable opinion and 30% unfavorable.[59]

Well, allow me to throw up a few caution flags before you invest your entire political capital into the metaphorical Trump Tower Jerusalem.

1. Unlike his four immediate predecessors, Trump didn't come into office with a comprehensive worldview of the Middle East. On other subjects he has sometimes changed course rather quickly, giving many foreign policy pundits a bad case of whiplash (clinics in DC noted a rash of such injuries among think tank experts on North Korea in the spring of 2018).

2. Trump is, as of this writing, a deeply unpopular President outside of his voter base. So the more strongly a particular policy is identified with him, the more negative response it may receive from those who might not care a lot about it except that "Trump supported it, therefore I oppose it." (Note that the exact same phenomenon occurred when Obama was president.) Given that the PIDS loathe Trump and his pro-Israel policies, they will happily try to make opposition to those policies a centerpiece to all anti-Trump activism. The most obvious example of that is the Women's March, whose leader

---

[59] https://www.brookings.edu/blog/order-from-chaos/2018/05/15/poll-jewish-israelis-love-trump/

Linda Sarsour has declared "Palestine" to be "the social justice cause of our generation." Given that Sarsour supports BDS and the exclusion of Zionists from human rights activism (as well as supporting Louis Farrakhan and his old-school "synagogue of Satan" anti-Semitism), it's a safe assumption that by "Palestine" she means "the eradication of the Jewish state." We don't want that to be the centerpiece of the anti-Trump "resistance."

3. Whether you believe they are valid or not, the multiple investigations into allegations of wrongdoing by members of the Trump Administration may indeed bear fruit. If his administration is brought down by scandal, all of his policies may become tainted by association—and those running against those policies will be supported by voter backlash. The ties connecting pro-Israel politics to Trump may be just as binding going downhill.

4. Trump's financial partners and contractors in his real estate and resort projects have a history of getting the short end of the Art of the Deal, and many former advisers have been jettisoned once they have either outlived their usefulness to him or were considered insufficiently loyal. We certainly don't want that to happen to Israel.

For these and many other reasons, having this president as the face of pro-Israel politics may not be a wise idea. Many staunch supporters of Israel did not vote for him, even as they support the steps he has taken to upgrade the US-Israel relationship. Supporting that relationship is based on advocating for specific policies and actions by the US government with respect to Israel. Opposing Trump does not automatically make one anti-Israel—that's what the PIDS would love to see, because it would allow them to gain mainstream credibility. <u>Don't help them out by taking the same position.</u>

For decades, the foundation of political activism for Israel has been to make the US-Israel relationship rest on bipartisan support. We are now in an era in which support for Israel is at risk of becoming like almost every other political issue: a partisan one, with each party facing towards its base rather than the center. Over the past 20 years, the Pew Research Center has asked the binary question "In the dispute between Israel and the Palestinians, which side do you sympathize with more?" The responses show that Republican support for Israel has reached record highs of support for Israel while amongst Democrats the numbers are approaching equality—and over the past 5 years self-described "liberal Democrats" support the Palestinians more.[60]

This poll question is quite flawed, reducing everything about Israel and the US-Israel relationship to this conflict, so it should not necessarily be viewed as a surrogate for American's views on Israel overall. Keep in mind as well that sympathizing with Palestinians is not necessarily the same as supporting BDS or Hamas. We, too, should sympathize with Palestinians, whose leadership has repeatedly condemned them to generations of sacrifice in the service of a fruitless jihad. But it does reflect a growing split between the two parties. And before you pat yourself on the back for being on the right side of this issue: if we approach the degree of polarization between Republicans and Democrats over Israel similar to that between the Conservative and Labour parties in the UK, it poses great risks for the US-Israel relationship, because at some point, the opposition party will gain power. And if you have demanded

---

[60] http://www.people-press.org/2018/01/23/republicans-and-democrats-grow-even-further-apart-in-views-of-israel-palestinians/

that all opposition to Trump be labeled as anti-Israel, you may be unfortunate enough to see that happen!

So you can put on your MAGA hat and enjoy the thought of riding to the (proposed) Trump train station in Jerusalem, but don't insist that all of your fellow Israel supporters get on board. They may choose an alternate mode of transportation, even to travel to see the US Embassy in Israel's capital.

If You Oppose Trump:

You don't even want to go into the building, much less up to the party in the penthouse. You are strongly opposed to Trump's policies on the environment, on reproductive rights, on immigration, and on the economy. You do like the actions that he's taken on Israel, but you have a hard time admitting that in public because you don't want to be seen as supporting him.

You've got a lot of company. Seventy percent of American Jews who voted in November of 2016 cast their ballots for Hillary Clinton. A New York Times opinion poll in January 2018 showed that only 26% of American Jews supported Trump—and that was after the announcement of the move of the US Embassy to Jerusalem.[61]

So where do you go? If you align with the completely anti-Trump "resistance" demonstrating outside, you'll find that the polar opposite of Trump is not Obama, or Hillary Clinton—

---

[61] https://www.jpost.com/American-Politics/On-Trump-Israeli-Jews-are-from-Mars-American-Jews-are-from-Venus-556606

it's Linda Sarsour and her "nothing is creepier than Zionism" fellow travelers. They've made it clear that supporters of Israel aren't welcome even when the issues being discussed are those on which Israel's example can be an excellent guide, such as LGBTQ rights, women's rights, and universal health care.

You still can, however, support specific actions and policies that Trump takes with regard to Israel. One quick thought experiment can serve you well here: "If Obama --or Hillary Clinton, had she won the Electoral College-- had done this, would I support it?" If the answer is yes, then follow the example of the Anti-Defamation League, which has been very vocal in its opposition to Trump's policies on immigration and his failure to respond more definitively to right-wing extremism, such as the neo-Nazi march in Charlottesville. Yet when it came to the opening of the US Embassy in Jerusalem, their statement specifically thanked the same president that they have otherwise heavily criticized: "We express our deep appreciation to the Trump Administration and the U.S. Government for making and implementing this long overdue move." Supporting Israel does not require that one endorse any other part of an Administration's agenda, or a Congressperson's voting record on any other issue.

Please understand as well that your Israeli cousins are viewing Trump's policies from a far different vantage point than you are. They are almost certainly not paying attention to the aspects of Trump's domestic policies that you oppose—whether it's taxes, judicial appointments, health care, or the environment.

Remember that things do change. No party remains in power forever. In the past 90 years, the candidate from the party of a retiring president won exactly once. (If you're on

"Jeopardy!" the correct response is "Who is George H.W. Bush?") So it's quite likely that after Trump, a Democrat will become President. It might be one who, in mirror image, will seek to undo all of Trump's policies; that candidate, and his or her base, may be distinctly unfriendly to Israel (oh, hi there, Bernie Sanders!). So your role here, even in the political wilderness, is critical. Pro-Israel Americans need to avoid having our support being exclusively identified with one party. Yes, the upswing in anti-Israel sentiment in the Democratic Party is real. We don't want candidates from that wing of the party winning primaries and potentially gaining elective office. So it's up to people like you to do the heavy lifting—to help ensure that Democrats who are elected are part of the mainstream on Israel, and not stand by while the PIDS try to take over the party-- as they have done successfully in Labour in the UK. There's a saying attributed to Lenin: "Probe with bayonets. If you encounter mush, proceed; if you encounter steel, withdraw." Be the steel.

Key Points:

1. Times change, and no one party is in power forever. Israel supporters should never put all their political eggs in one basket.

2. You can support pro-Israel policies of a president even if you disagree with him (or her) on many other issues.

Chapter 13: Now It's Your Turn

Zionist Pugs

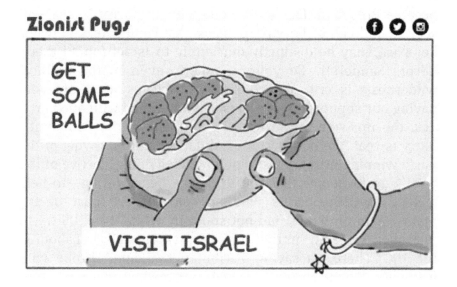

You are not obliged to complete the task, but neither are you free to evade it.

-- Rabbi Tarfon, 2nd century

Now that you've made it this far, what's next? Sorry, there's no coupon to send in to the International Zionist Conspiracy to get a certificate of completion. As I pointed out in Chapter One, this book is just a starting point. And if it has stimulated your interest in learning more, then the "Resources" page at the end of this chapter is a good continuation.

And now, when you come across the PIDS tabling on campus, or gathering signatures for yet another "boycott Israel" initiative at the local food co-op or farmer's market, you can utilize the information and the techniques described here to expose their lies and give their intended audience the real story.

My own experience, and that of other Israel advocates across the country, is that PIDS absolutely hate any public challenge to their distorted view of Israel. In part, that's a natural response—if you don't have the facts on your side, you don't want to have to defend your position. So the act of simply pointing out their errors—calmly, occupying the rhetorical as well as the moral high ground—is enough to make them reach for their antacids.

You don't even need to be face to face with PIDS to be able to counter their attempts to turn public opinion against Israel. Write letters to the editor, especially if you live in a smaller community where people still read a newspaper to get local news, or if you're on campus where the letters section provides a space for public dialogue. Not every letter gets published, but the more letters received with a specific point of view, the more likely the opinion editor will be to run at least some of them. It's very important to pay attention to the rules of the newspaper—many newspapers will not run a letter unless they contact you by phone to verify that it was your letter, so if they ask you to include a phone number, do it. And some newspapers are extremely strict about the word count. If they say 200 words, they mean 200 words. So you might be proud of that 658 word essay you sent to your local paper, but nobody else will get to read it!

Another way to take action is to show up at pro-Israel public gatherings (or to counter an anti-Israel protest) in your community or on your campus. Depending upon where you live, such events might occur only on rare occasions or, in places like the San Francisco Bay Area, they can be daily occurrences, as they were during Operation Pillar of Defense in 2012. Showing up, even just to stand with an Israeli flag or pro-peace sign against the PIDS, is important for several reasons. It shows that supporters of Israel are not willing to cede the "public square" to PIDS who are busy promoting lies such as "genocide in Gaza." It gives Israel supporters a chance to talk to members of the public who are part of the great majority that doesn't know much about the issue. Most importantly, the news media will almost always ensure that they give coverage to people who are (literally) on opposite sides of the street at a demonstration. It's very important in such cases to have designated media spokespeople who are able to answer the question that any reporter (whether print, TV or radio) will ask: "Why are you here today?" And they need to answer it directly, succinctly, and in 30 seconds or less if they are dealing with TV or radio—because that's the longest soundbite that you will get. I've done this on local TV news over a dozen times, and my answer almost always sounds like this:

"We're here today to stand up for Israel's right to exist as the state of the Jewish people. Israel wants peace, but it's facing enemies who call for its elimination and who launch rockets at millions of Israeli civilians. Israel has offered a Palestinian state but has been answered with calls for jihad and genocide." And if you are countering a group of PIDS protesting with their "Palestine will be free from the river to the sea" and "intifada, intifada" chants, you can add "Those on the other side of the street are calling for eternal war. Those of us here are calling for peace."

StandWithUs (the organization which I represent in the San Francisco Bay Area) has comprehensive resources for organizing public rallies as well as a wealth of educational information about Israel that is useful for outreach on both the campus and in the community. There are downloadable signs that can be printed up at a copy shop with a large format printer, and flyers that are useful to hand out to the public. All of these are freely available at www.standwithus.com. They have chapters in many major cities across the country, and student representatives on many prominent university campuses. StandWithUs has also taken the pro-Israel case to the public with advertisements on transit systems in cities such as San Francisco, Seattle, Houston, Washington DC and Vancouver.

One of the best ways to counter PIDS who protest at a store carrying Israeli goods is to organize a "buy-cott." Just as the PIDS hate to have their lies challenged in public, they also quickly learn that their calls for boycotts often result in communities organizing to support the store and buy the products. During a 2009 campaign against the Trader Joe's chain (which carries several Israeli food products), many local communities organized weekly "buy-cott" trips to Trader Joe's stores—some of which continued many months later! When PIDS see their efforts result in greater purchases of Israeli products, they cease using that tactic.

Contacting elected officials is a vitally important component of advocacy. Senators and Representatives all have contact forms on their official websites—after the anthrax bioterrorism incidents in 2001, the federal government is not keen on receiving envelopes from the general public in the Capitol or the White House. AIPAC, the American Israel Public Affairs Committee, is the most important Israel advocacy organization with regard to Federal legislative affairs—so effective that it is often represented by PIDS as the leader of a nefarious secret society ("The Israel Lobby") that acts throughout federal and even state and local governments. In fact it is an organization of American citizens that openly-- and entirely legally-- urges its members to communicate with Senators and Representatives to support the US-Israel relationship. AIPAC neither endorses nor rates candidates for Congress or any other elected office. AIPAC hosts speaking events around the country and also has a very large Policy Conference in Washington DC every year, which features speeches from high level government officials from both parties, educational sessions, and going to Capitol Hill to meet with Congressional representatives.

If you join AIPAC, you will receive action alerts which will ask you to contact your Members of Congress regarding specific legislation or initiatives. It's important that when you contact your elected representatives, you make it very clear what you are specifically asking them to do and why (you will receive talking points in the action alerts). Don't confuse a Congressional staff member with an e-mail relating to a specific piece of legislation that isn't clear about which side you are supporting: "YES" or "NO." And you don't need to write a three page letter on the topic—something brief and to the point is more likely to get read in its entirety.

The largest pro-Israel organization in the United States is not AIPAC, but rather Christians United for Israel (CUFI). CUFI works to educate the Christian community about Israel and also holds a large annual meeting in Washington DC similar to AIPAC's Policy Conference.

What about J Street? J Street is a newer organization founded in 2008, whose members also seek to influence US government policy towards Israel. J Street specifically lobbies for or against legislation based on whether they believe that it will promote or hinder the two-state solution, regardless of what policy the government of Israel has adopted. J Street has been the focus of much controversy within the pro-Israel community because of positions it has taken against Israeli government actions as well as Israeli proposals in negotiations with the Palestinians, and because of anti-Israel statements made by some of the candidates that it has endorsed. During the debate about the Iran nuclear deal, J Street stood alone (among organizations describing themselves as pro-Israel) in strongly endorsing the deal, which was opposed not only by the government of Israel but also by opposition leaders Isaac Herzog and Yair Lapid. All of this leads to the inescapable conclusion that there are many potholes and malfunctioning traffic signals on J Street; the road might be heading in the right direction, but perhaps detours are advised.

There is one more essential ingredient to your ability, and your motivation, to advocate for Israel: if you have not yet traveled to Israel, GO. See the land and the people for yourself. See the historical record of the Jewish people engraved all over the land of our ancestors. Experience the vibrancy of everyday life in a country that—despite repeated attempts to destroy it militarily and now to isolate it economically and politically—has reconstituted the Jewish nation in its homeland as a center of democracy and freedom, in a region where both of those values have been extraordinarily difficult to establish.

Then come back and stand up even more strongly for the right of the Jewish people to sing the words from Hatikvah, Israel's national anthem, "Hatikvah bat sh'not alpayim, L'hiyot am hofshe b'artzenu, eretz Tziyon v'Yerushalayim": "the hope of two thousand years, to live as a free people, in our own land, the land of Zion and Jerusalem."

RESOURCES:

Books

The Case for Israel by Alan Dershowitz

Why I Am A Zionist by Gil Troy

Myths and Facts by Mitchell Bard

The Promise of Israel by Daniel Gordis

1948 by Benny Morris

Letters to My Palestinian Neighbor by Yossi Klein Halevi

Organizations

StandWithUs www.standwithus.com Twitter @standwithus, www.facebook.com/StandWithUs/

AIPAC www.aipac.org Twitter @AIPAC, www.facebook.com/aipac/

Christians United for Israel www.cufi.org Twitter @ cufi, www.facebook.com/ChristiansUnitedforIsrael

JIMENA (Jews Indigenous to the Middle East and North Africa) www.jimena.org Twitter @JIMENA_Voice, www.facebook.com/JimenaJewsIndigenousToTheMiddleEastAndNorthAfrica

NGO Monitor https://www.ngo-monitor.org/ Twitter @ngomonitor, https://www.facebook.com/NgoMonitor/

News from Israel

The Times of Israel (www.timesofisrael.com)

Jerusalem Post (www.jpost.com)

YnetNews (www.ynetnews.com)

Israel HaYom (www.israelhayom.com)

Blogs

Elder of Ziyon www.elderofziyon.blogspot.com, Twitter @elderofziyon Israelly Cool www.israellycool.com Twitter @israellycool

Divest This! www.divestthis.com Twitter @divestthis ProIsraelBayBloggers www.proisraelbaybloggers.blogspot.com

The Israel Advocacy Handbook http://zionism-israel.com/Israel_advocacy.pdf

Index:

About the Author:

Dr. Michael Harris is one of the founders of San Francisco Voice for Israel, which is now the Bay Area chapter of StandWithUs. Founded in 2004, SF Voice for Israel has countered anti-Israel demonstrations, to provide the public and the media with an alternative to the lies being promoted by organizations such as International ANSWER and Jewish Voice for Peace. It has also done proactive public outreach at community events and brought pro-Israel speakers to the Bay Area. As part of StandWithUs, founded in 2001, the group is now part of a worldwide Israel education organization with chapters across the US as well as in Canada, Europe and Israel.

In his role with the group, Dr. Harris has made appearances on radio shows (both in the US and in Israel) and television news reports as a local spokesperson, countering misinformation about Israel. He's given speeches to large groups at synagogues, churches, political organizations and senior citizen centers throughout the San Francisco Bay Area. In addition, he's been in the trenches, standing up for Israel against anti-Israel demonstrators on the streets of San Francisco and Oakland for over a decade. In his spare time, he is a pediatrician in Marin County, California.

Made in the USA
Columbia, SC
30 June 2022

62565600R00124